Miracle of '48

Miracle

HARRY TRUMAN'S MAJOR CAMPAIG

of '48

PEECHES & SELECTED WHISTLE-STOPS

EDITED BY Steve Neal

FOREWORD BY Robert V. Remini

Southern Illinois University Press CARBONDALE

FOR IRV KUPCINET AND GEORGE M. ELSEY

Book and jacket design by Richard Hendel.

Library of Congress Cataloging-in-Publication Data

Truman, Harry S., 1884–1972.
 Miracle of '48 : Harry Truman's major campaign speeches and
selected whistle-stops / edited by Steve Neal.
  p. cm.
  1. United States—Politics and government—1945–1953.
2. Presidents—United States—Election—1948. 3. Political
campaigns—United States—History—20th century. 4. Speeches,
addresses, etc., American. I. Title: Miracle of forty-eight. II. Neal,
Steve, 1949– III. Title.

 E742.5 .T65 2003
 324.973′0918—dc21
 ISBN 0-8093-2557-8 (alk. paper)   2003010658

Contents

Foreword

Steve Neal is an outstanding journalist and historian to whom we are deeply indebted for providing these speeches that reveal new facets of Harry Truman's remarkable career. A noted biographer and essayist, Neal has generally focused his attention on the 1940s and 1950s but has always been conscious of their relevance to the present and the need to make Americans aware of the connection and its importance. In this book he has assembled a series of documents about the election of 1948 that can help us better understand one of the most misunderstood and reviled presidents in our history.

Personally, I shall never forget the presidential election of 1948. It was one of the most humiliating experiences of my entire academic life. I had just been employed as an assistant professor to teach American history to freshmen at Fordham University, having just received my master's degree from Columbia University, where I studied with such outstanding historians as Dumas Malone, Richard Hofstadter, Henry Steele Commager, and Alan Nevins. I was continuing my studies toward a doctorate in history at Columbia but had decided that I would try to get a job where I could share my expanded knowledge of the American past with young students recently graduated from high school. More to the point I was getting married, and I thought it about time I started earning a living.

To my surprise, the students who faced me in the classroom at Fordham were not young and recent high school graduates but, like me, were veterans of World War II who were taking advantage of the GI Bill of Rights to pursue their education. Many of them were much older than I and had families. Still I was not about to be intimidated by their age. After all, who had the master's degree?

Thus, in the fall of 1948, when the presidential campaign went into full swing, I decided to make what I thought was a valid historical point by predicting that Harry S. Truman could not possibly win reelection. And this wrongheaded prediction wasn't prompted by the many polls that regularly appeared in the media predicting his defeat or the fact that the president was widely perceived as unpopular and lacking respect from the electorate. I had recourse to the nation's past to justify my conclusion. I had history! So I pointed out to my students that in the presidential election of 1860 the nation faced a similar situation when the Democratic Party split into two segments and as a result forfeited the election to the Republican candidate, Abraham Lincoln. And Lincoln won a majority of electoral votes, even though those votes came from a single section of the country.

The crucial question that animated the contest was slavery. For decades the nation had agonized over this "peculiar institution," as it was called, and had searched for a compromise that could resolve the problem and spare the country a bloody civil war. By the mid-1850s the tired and bankrupt Whig Party had all but disappeared. In its place the Republican Party had emerged in a new attempt to address the country's looming sectional crisis. The Democratic Party held its nominating convention in Charleston, North Carolina, in April 1860 and split over naming a suitable candidate and platform. Southern delegates walked out and at a separate convention nominated John C. Breckinridge of Kentucky while northerner Democrats meeting in Baltimore named Stephen A. Douglas of Illinois. As the nominee of the Republican Party, Lincoln had the solid backing of those who opposed slavery. Then a fourth party appeared: the Constitutional Union Party, made up of former Whigs and those who rightly feared that Lincoln's election would precipitate secession by the southern states. John Bell of Tennessee was put forward for the presidency by this party.

The fracturing of the Democratic Party in 1860, I remember pontificating to my students, proved to be a certain formula for disaster. And that formula had been repeated in 1948, when the Dixiecrats bolted the party and chose Strom Thurmond as their candidate, while those fearful that the cold war could be ignited into a hot one nominated Henry A. Wallace. Truman was left with what remained of the Democratic Party.

The 1860 election ended with the triumph of Lincoln, when he garnered 180 electoral votes to 72 for Breckinridge, 39 for Bell, and 12 for Douglas. Although Douglas won only Missouri and a portion of New Jersey's electoral vote, he rolled up a large popular vote, both northern and southern, receiving 1,383,000 to Lincoln's 1,866,000. The other candidates did not come anywhere near these totals.

It seemed clear to me in 1948 that history was about to repeat itself. I should have known better. History does not repeat itself. Truman knew that. He was a longtime devotee of American history and had read extensively in the subject. He had a feel for this nation's past and how it had evolved. He knew that the situation in 1948 was not the same as in 1860. He knew and firmly believed that he could win the election, impossible though it seemed at the time. He had a sense of the needs and wishes of the American electorate, and by reading these speeches, so lovingly collected and edited by Steve Neal, one can understand how this remarkable man Truman achieved his astounding victory. One also glimpses some of the reasons why Truman was such a superb leader and why he has risen in the minds of American historians to rank among our near-great presidents, even though he was reviled by many of his contemporaries as a hopeless incompetent. His achievement was indeed a miracle, as Steve Neal contends, and provides a lesson that young and old historians would do well to ponder.

Robert V. Remini

Acknowledgments

I am indebted to the Harry S. Truman Presidential Library for making available the original texts of these speeches, including numerous drafts of President Truman's major addresses. An indispensable source is *Public Papers of the Presidents: Harry S. Truman 1948* (Washington: U.S. Government Printing Office, 1964), which contains the speeches delivered by HST. Thanks to reference librarian Elizabeth Safly of the Truman Library, who encouraged me to undertake this volume and generously provided her recommendations of the president's speeches. I am also grateful for the help of archivists Dennis Bilger and Randy Sowell. Clifton Truman Daniel, the president's grandson, who has added to his family's legacy of public service, was invaluable in sharing memories of his grandfather and offering suggestions for this volume.

It is no accident that Truman speaks across the generations and is among the more widely quoted American presidents. As this volume demonstrates, he championed principles of economic and social justice and concern for the less fortunate that are ageless and still relevant in today's world. In shaping his message for the 1948 election, he had the assistance of a remarkable team of speechwriters that included the incomparable George McKee Elsey, Charles S. Murphy, Clark M. Clifford, Jonathan Daniels, and C. Girard Davidson. They helped Truman achieve the Miracle of '48.

I am grateful to Rick Stetter, director of Southern Illinois University Press for his enthusiasm and assistance. Former senator Paul Simon, director of the SIU Public Policy Institute, associate director Mike Lawrence, and their distinguished colleague John Jackson have also been most helpful and provided helpful suggestions.

Thanks to my editors at the *Chicago Sun-Times*—Michael Cooke, John Cruickshank, and Steve Huntley.

My wife, Susan, and my daughters, Erin and Shannon, are a constant source of support and allowed me to have the time to complete this project. I am most grateful.

Harry S. Truman. (Marion Carpenter, courtesy Truman Library)

Introduction

If Harry Truman had decided not to seek the presidency in 1948, nobody would have blamed him. For three years, the weight of the world had hung on his shoulders. He had led the grand alliance to its final victory in World War II. In May 1948 he began rebuilding war-ravaged Europe through the Marshall Plan. He was a fighter for freedom. When Stalin threatened to starve West Berlin that June in the first major battle of the cold war, Truman refused to back down. He responded with the airlift that ultimately broke the blockade and thwarted Soviet expansionism.

No other American president was required to make so many fateful decisions in so brief a time. Though Truman is now recognized as one of our greatest presidents, he was underappreciated and underestimated in the election year of 1948. After sixteen years of Democratic government, a great many Americans were in the mood for change. Following the 1946 midterm elections in which Republicans captured the House and the Senate, one of the Democratic Party's more respected senators urged the embattled president to step down in favor of a Republican.

All the odds were against his reelection. A Gallup poll in the spring of 1948 showed that only about a third of the American people approved of the president's job performance. What made his situation even more perilous was the splintering of the Democratic Party. Its left and right wings had broken off, leaving the party more divided than at any time since the Civil War. Former vice president Henry A. Wallace, who resented Truman for replacing him on the Democratic ticket in 1944, asserted that the new president's foreign policy was unfair to the Soviet Union. As the third-party candidate of the left, Wallace was expected to attract as many as three million votes. Meanwhile, the president's bold plan to outlaw racial segregation was bitterly spurned by states'-rights Democrats in the South. The Dixiecrats nominated South Carolina governor Strom Thurmond as their presidential candidate, and he was expected to carry at least four states that had been traditionally Democratic. Third-party candidacies would doom the reelection hopes of three other twentieth-century presidents (Taft, Carter, and Bush) and, in 1968, resulted in the Democratic loss of the White House.

The disunity of the Democratic Party and the expected losses to Wallace and Thurmond were among the reasons that the odds against Truman's re-election were 20 to 1. There were more than a few Democratic politicians who hoped that he would choose retirement over certain defeat.

But Truman, who believed that he was doing a good job, wasn't a quitter. "I had to run again and establish the Democratic Party as a national party, not one just representing certain elements," he said years later. "I was going to run if I got only one vote — my own."

At the Republican National Convention, the president was dismissed by its keynote speaker as "a gone goose." The Republicans were fielding their strongest ticket in a generation and appeared to be on the verge of reclaiming power. It would take an extraordinary effort to stop them. The GOP, which had won seven out of the nine presidential elections before Franklin D. Roosevelt and would win four of six presidential elections after Truman, was set for a restoration.

The shadow of FDR was also threatening Truman's reelection. Though Truman was widely regarded as a good and decent man, there was a feeling among some of Roosevelt's associates that he wasn't big enough for the job. Eleanor Roosevelt declined to endorse him for renomination and worked behind the scenes to stop him. Three of her sons led a movement to dump Truman. A month before the Philadelphia convention, the president confronted Jimmy Roosevelt: "Your father asked me to take this job. I didn't want it. I was happy in the Senate. But your father asked me to take it and I took it. And if your father knew what you are doing to me, he would turn over in his grave. But get this straight: whether you like it or not, I am going to be the next president of the United States."

That view wasn't shared by many of the party faithful at the 1948 Democratic National Convention. Senator Alben Barkley of Kentucky, who gave a rip-snorting keynote speech, got such an ovation that he was hopeful that the delegates might turn to him as an alternative choice. The president didn't depart for Philadelphia until John Snyder assured him that the nomination was locked up. Supreme Court Justice William O. Douglas, who had wanted to be FDR's running mate in 1944, declined Truman's offer of the vice presidency. Douglas confided to a friend that he didn't want to be "number two man to a number two man." Barkley, one of the Democratic Party's great warhorses, was Truman's second choice and gladly accepted.

The president didn't get to deliver his acceptance speech until after 2 A.M. Before he spoke, fifty "doves of peace," which were actually white pigeons, were released from under a floral Liberty Bell. What followed was from out of a Marx Brothers movie. One bird dropped dead to the floor, and others inflicted some damage on the clothes of the delegates. When a pigeon landed on the rostrum, convention chairman Sam Rayburn managed to capture it and sent it flying over the crowd.

Then the president got down to business. In his acceptance speech, he outlined the differences between the major parties. He spoke about the Democratic legacy as the party of the people and defined the opposition as the party of privilege. The GOP "still helps the rich and sticks a knife in the back of the poor," he asserted. Truman went on: "The Republican platform comes out for slum clearance and low-rental housing. I have been trying to get them to pass this housing bill ever since they met the first time, and it is still resting in the rules committee. . . . The Republican platform urges expanding and increasing Social Security benefits . . . and yet when they had the opportunity they took 750,000 people off the Social Security rolls."

Then came the showstopper. "My duty as president requires that I use every means within my power to get the laws the people need in such important matters, and I am therefore calling this Congress back into special session on the twenty-sixth of July," Truman declared. He would call the GOP's bluff by testing the sincerity of its platform.

Thomas E. Dewey, the Republican presidential nominee, sought to remain above the fray by ignoring Truman and distancing himself from the GOP Congress. All of the polls indicated that Dewey would be the next president of the United States. When Truman and Dewey shared the platform at the dedication of New York's Idlewild Airport that summer, the fates were still against the president. Dewey spoke without interruption, while Truman's remarks were drowned out by planes.

Though eighteen years younger than Truman, Dewey had been a national figure since the early 1930s. He had gained fame and prominence as New York's racket-busting federal prosecutor and later as district attorney. After he sent notorious gangsters and corrupt politicians to jail, Dewey's accomplishments were celebrated in movies and a popular radio series. As the governor of New York since 1942, he had established himself as a formidable vote-getter and skillful administrator. As the 1944 Republican presidential nominee, Dewey had given FDR his toughest challenge. After choosing California governor Earl Warren as his running mate, Dewey was viewed as all but invincible in 1948.

But Truman wasn't ready to concede. Soon after the Philadelphia convention, he inspired his White House staff with a pep talk that gave them a glimmer of hope. "We are going to win," he said. "I expect to travel all over the country and talk at every whistle-stop. We are going to be on the road most of the time from Labor Day to the end of the campaign. It's going to be tough on everybody, but that's the way it's got to be. I know I can take it. I'm only afraid that I'll kill some of my staff — and I like you all very much and I don't want to do that."

He understood that the whole concept of a campaign was to motivate the voter and to galvanize support for the candidate and the political party. He believed that it was possible to change the way that people thought and that having the better argument was the best way to win elections. The president fervently believed in the Democratic Party's heritage as the party that gave voice to the powerless. "There never was a nonpartisan in politics," he once noted. "A man cannot be a nonpartisan and be effective in a political party. When he's in any party — he's partisan, he's got to be."

Dewey, whose record as governor of New York had been a good one, was an elusive target. But Truman sought to turn the 1948 election into a referendum on the Republican-controlled 80th Congress, which had rejected his domestic policies. When the special session declined to take action on his initiatives, he denounced the "do-nothing 80th Congress" and aligned the Democratic Party with social change. In foreign policy, the Republican Congress had been generally supportive of the administration. Truman, though, had used his veto sixty-two times to thwart conservative GOP legislation. Even before the Democratic convention, he found audiences responding favorably to his attacks on "the good-for-nothing 80th Congress." By portraying the election as the Republican Party against the working people of the United States, the president ran as if he was the challenger.

At the same time, he used his incumbency to establish special connections with important constituencies. As the product of farm country and the first Democratic president from west of the Mississippi, he understood the importance of the family farm and took steps to protect it. The farmers knew that he was on their side. His veto of the Taft-Hartley Labor Act brought organized labor into the 1948 campaign in record numbers. He gained support from Jewish Americans and others with his de facto recognition of Israel in May 1948. His executive orders in July that ended segregation in the armed services and in the federal government were regarded by African Americans as milestones in the struggle for black equality. Truman had done more for civil rights in three years than Roosevelt had in twelve. In response to a letter from a white southern veteran of World War I who disagreed with the plan to outlaw segregation, the president answered: "If that ends up in my failure to be reelected, that failure will be in a good cause."

Whether or not that would be the reason, almost no one gave Truman any chance of winning. In political campaigns, the polls are often a self-fulfilling prophecy. If there is a perception that an election is going to be lopsided, large numbers of voters often stay home. It is much more difficult for candidates to raise contributions if the polls indicate that they have no chance. Truman's biggest challenge as a candidate was overcoming the consultant in August: "Why does the Republican candidate want to spend any money? The results are a foregone conclusion."

Many Democrats shared that opinion. Some of the party's more reliable contributors shunned Truman. Wall Street's Bernard Baruch, who had been an ally of FDR's and Woodrow Wilson's, declined to serve as finance chairman in 1948. The Texas millionaire Jesse H. Jones, who had served in Roosevelt's cabinet, turned down an invitation to head the finance committee and then endorsed Dewey. Even in Kansas City, Truman got rejections from the Kemper brothers, who headed two of the largest banks and had been active in Democratic politics.

"People didn't think Truman was going to win — so why back a losing horse? That's why he didn't get any money," the president's aide Matt Connelly recalled in his oral history. "Nobody thought he was going to win."

On more than one occasion, radio broadcasts of the president's speeches were cut short because there wasn't enough money to pay for the airtime. More than a half dozen times, the president's friends would have to take up a collection to pay the railroad so that Truman's campaign train could be moved out of town. "We'd go into a town like Chicago. We wouldn't know how to get the train out," Connelly recalled. "We didn't have the money to pay the freight." The president himself had to ask several friends to come through with enough funding to get his train moving out of Washington's Union Station.

The 1948 campaign marked the end of the whistle-stop era. It was the last time that both major presidential nominees would wage their campaigns on the railroads. Each of the trains reflected the personalities of the candidates. Dewey's campaign was the more smoothly run operation. But Truman put on the better show, and even though he was being written off as a loser, there were early hints that the people didn't like being taken for granted.

On the first stop of an early campaign swing, a crowd of more than four thousand greeted the president at Rock Island, Illinois — at 5:45 in the morning. William Bray, a veteran of Democratic national politics who worked in the 1948 campaign, told the president: "In spite of the polls there are a lot of people who have not made up their minds and are willing to listen, and that's all we can ask for."

Later in the day, Truman spoke before more than eighty thousand farmers at the national plowing contest in Dexter, Iowa. With vivid imagery, he alleged that the 80th Congress had "stuck a pitchfork in the farmer's backs." What it had done was to slash federal grain-storage capacity by more than 80 percent. The farmers, who had produced a record crop that year, had no place to store it and were forced to sell wheat and corn at below-market prices.

When the Republicans attacked the Truman administration for shoring up farm prices through price supports, it helped Truman's cause. "Only with a Democratic president and a Democratic Congress can you be sure that you will get a square deal on prices," the president told farm audiences.

Dewey, who seldom lost his cool during the campaign, made an unfortunate comment in downstate Illinois when his "Victory Special" train accidentally backed up and narrowly missed the crowd. "That's the first lunatic I've had for an engineer," Dewey exclaimed. "He should probably be shot at sunrise, but we'll let him off this time since no one was hurt." Those words became a rallying cry in union halls across the country.

Truman enjoyed campaigning more than Dewey, and though Truman was older, he exuded more vitality. Charles G. Ross, Truman's press secretary, recalled that when a bottle of soda pop fell off the window ledge in the private railroad car and drenched the president's trousers, he didn't have time to change "and went to the platform with his trousers dripping." When a crowd of several thousand gathered at Missoula at 1 A.M., Ross woke up the president. "He put on a dressing gown over his pajamas and went out and chatted with his visitors for ten minutes," Ross recalled.

Three weeks before the election, *Newsweek* polled fifty political experts. Their verdict was unanimous. Dewey couldn't lose. Forty-three of the poll's respondents listed a "general desire for change" as the most decisive factor in the 1948 election. Thirty-six also said that voters thought Truman wasn't big enough for the job. More than a third of those interviewed said that the president couldn't overcome the Democratic Party's three-way split.

When they were asked whose election would be in the national interest, Truman got just seven votes. But Truman told his aide Clark Clifford not to worry about the gloomy forecast. "I know every one of them," the president said of *Newsweek*'s distinguished panel, "and not one of them has enough sense to pour sand into a rat hole."

But few doubted the poll. The *New York Times* called Dewey's triumph "a foregone conclusion." The then liberal *New York Post* suggested that the Democrats "might as well immediately concede the election to Dewey." The *Christian Science Monitor* declared that Dewey's election is "as certain as anything can be in the course of American politics."

Only 15 percent of the nation's newspapers supported Truman's reelection. The *St. Louis Post-Dispatch* lamented that Truman did not have the "stature, the vision, the social and economic grasp, the sense of history required to lead the nation in a time of crisis."

Mrs. Truman had grave doubts about her husband's chances. Clifford thought that his chances were remote. Tom Evans believed that "it was a cinch he was going to lose, he just couldn't win." Truman insisted otherwise, though he was philosophical about his chances in private conversation. "I'm out slugging, doing the best I can," he told Irv Kupcinet of the *Chicago Sun-Times*. "No man can do more."

One of the more memorable cartoons that fall was drawn by C. K. Berryman of the *Washington Star*. It showed Truman glumly looking at a bulletin board with reports of Dewey's inevitable landslide. A strutting Dewey, holding his lapels, chortled: "What's the use of going through with the election?"

But the people had other ideas. Instead of a landslide, the 1948 presidential election turned out to be the closest in thirty-two years. When President Truman went to bed on election night, the outcome was uncertain. Dewey had led in some of the early returns and carried the megastates of the industrial Northeast. Thurmond won four states in the Deep South. But the president was showing surprising strength in the farm states and in the West and would win five states that Dewey had carried over FDR in 1944. Blacks had voted for Truman by 9 to 1. The undecided vote, which traditionally goes against the incumbent, broke in favor of the president. When all the votes were counted, it turned out that Truman had achieved the greatest upset in American history. Not one poll or political analyst had predicted this outcome.

The image of President Truman gleefully flaunting the premature headline of the *Chicago Tribune* proclaiming Dewey's victory is the most famous blunder in the history of journalism. "This is one for the books," HST exclaimed with that wonderful smile as he held up the "Dewey Beats Truman" front page. Other newspapers and magazines also got it wrong. But what made this so exhilarating was that the *Tribune* was the voice of midwestern Republicanism and isolationism. Earlier that fall, when the president had attacked "the world's greatest newspaper," the *Tribune* shot back in an editorial that Truman could add his name "to the long list of political crooks and incompetents who have regarded the *Tribune* as first among their foes."

How did the *Tribune* blow the election? Arthur Sears Henning, the newspaper's chief Washington correspondent, finished writing his analysis of Dewey's victory by midmorning on election day. Because the newspaper's printers were on strike, deadlines were pushed forward by a half day for the early edition. Henning, who had covered national politics for forty years, was so confident in his judgment that he reported Dewey's election through the newspaper's first six editions. Henning finally conceded in the seventh and last edition that "at 6 A.M. on Wednesday morning, the presidential race remained uncertain."

The headline "Dewey Defeats Truman" was changed in the third edition to "GOP Wins White House." The fourth edition was revised to "Dewey Ahead." Colonel Robert R. McCormick, who smoldered when his newspaper was held up to international ridicule, made it known that heads would roll. Henning and his managing editor were dumped for their roles in the great mistake of 1948. But the photograph lives on as the most enduring image of a triumphant underdog.

In looking back on the 1948 election, Earl Warren, who was Dewey's running mate, said that Truman won "because he was such a plain and simple man, going out on his own, on a whirlwind trip to talk with the people, whereas Governor Dewey was talking at them, and that's a great difference."

Of the many letters received by President Truman after his great upset, none summed it up better than this one: "The political history of the United States reveals many unusual developments, but certainly at no point does it record a greater accomplishment than yours, that can be traced so clearly to the stark courage and fighting heart of a single man." It was signed Dwight D. Eisenhower.

Major Speeches and Selected Whistle-Stop Remarks of 1948

JUNE 4

Rear Platform Remarks
Crestline, Ohio (Noon)

Thank you. Thank you very much. It is a very great pleasure for me to see you out here this morning. It is a pleasure to me. You know how intriguing it is, and helpful it is, for the president to get away from the White House and get to see the people as they are.

The president, you know, is virtually in jail. He goes from his study to his office and from his office to his study, and he has to have guards there all the time. And they do a good job, too — I am not criticizing the guards — but when you get out and see people and find out what people are thinking about, you can do a better job as president of the United States.

It has been a most pleasant trip, so far. This is the biggest gathering we have had anywhere. I understand that this is top of the world in Ohio.

On this nonpartisan, bipartisan trip that we are taking here, I understand there are a whole lot of Democrats present, too. It is a pleasure to have been able to see the governor. I know he is going to be the next governor of Ohio.

★ Fort Wayne, Indiana (2:20 P.M.)

Mr. Chairman, ladies and gentlemen of Fort Wayne:

It is a very great pleasure indeed for me to have a chance to stop at Fort Wayne. I have always, all my life, been an admirer of "Mad Anthony" Wayne. You know, Mad Anthony had a dictionary without the word "can't" in it. Whenever he was given a job to do, he did it. These Northwest Territories are very much beholden to him for being a part of the greatest republic in the world.

In his day, people were thinking just as they are now. They were anxious for peace and security, and they themselves contributed to making that peace and security. They usually had their own squirrel rifle up over the door, the bag full of powder and shot, and a King James version of the Bible. It took all those things to make this great community what it is now.

Now people are asking today: will there be a permanent peace? I can say to you categorically that there will be a permanent peace if the United States of America assumes the role that God Almighty intended the United States of America to assume in 1920.

There are three things necessary for peace in the world. The first is to have the United Nations to work as the United Nations Charter intends it to work, and that is what we have been working for ever since that charter was agreed to.

The next most important thing right now is the success of the European recovery program. If the sixteen nations that agreed at Paris to the European recovery program are encouraged and we carry out the agreements which we made with them without stint, Europe will recover and we will have peace in Europe. It is just as necessary that we have peace in Asia as it is to have it in Europe, and since we are the leaders in world government, we will see that we carry out those agreements to the letter. And I sincerely hope that the Congress will carry out the agreement that was made by these sixteen nations to the letter, and not quibble on it.

The next most important thing we are faced with is the necessity that we have the strength to maintain that peace. In November 1945, I requested the Congress to give us a universal training program so that we could be in a position, after our demobilization, to maintain the peace. In January 1946 and again in 1946, and in January 1947 and again in 1947, and last November and last January, I asked Congress for the same thing, for the same reason. We must be strong enough to maintain the peace if we expect to have peace in the world. If we did not have a police force in Fort Wayne, capable of enforcing the city ordinances, you wouldn't have any peace. That's all I am asking for; that's all we need. And I sincerely hope that this Congress will give us that temporary draft and universal training that are necessary to keep this country in the lead. That means peace in the world.

If those three things which I called to your attention are carried through to the logical conclusion, there will be peace, and there will be permanent peace, and there will be prosperity in all the world, for there are enough resources on this old globe to give everybody his fair share, and that's all the United States government is working for.

Thank you very much.

JUNE 5

Address at the Reunion of the 35th Division
Ak-sar-ben Coliseum, Omaha (7:15 P.M.)

Mr. Chairmen, distinguished guests, ladies and gentlemen:

I am very happy to be back again tonight with the men of the 35th Division — one of the greatest fighting outfits this country ever had!

It is good to meet again with old friends who were my buddies in the First World War. I am proud, also, to meet the young men who brought new glory to the division in the Second World War.

The story of the 35th Division is to me an example of one of the finest features of our democracy. This was a National Guard division. Here were trained civilians, ready to come to the defense of their country. When the need arose, these men, and thousands of other National Guardsmen throughout the nation, answered the call — and answered on time. I won't go so far as to say that the National Guard won the war. But I will say that if it had not been for the National Guard and the reserve components of our armed forces, the story would have been quite different.

You and I have shared the privilege of serving in the defense of our country. Now that the fighting is over, we have an equally great privilege to serve in another cause. In time of war, we worked together for victory. Now we must work together to secure the peace and the blessings which that victory has made possible.

This time, we must make sure that the tragic events that followed the First World War are not repeated. Looking back, the mistakes that were made in the years following the First World War are so obvious, and their consequences were so terrible, that there can be no excuse for repeating them.

Fortunately, we have learned from that bitter experience. After the First World War, the chief hope for keeping the peace was the League of Nations — the great dream of Woodrow Wilson. But shortsighted men in the United States Senate blocked our entry into that league, and it never recovered from that blow.

This time, the United States took a leading part in organizing the United Nations. In spite of the difficulties it has had, the United Nations is working. And we are determined to make it succeed!

In addition to learning that we must cooperate with other nations to keep the peace, we have learned something also about how to maintain our prosperity at home — at least, most of us have. As a result of the boom and bust of the 1920s and the 1930s, we have learned that the welfare of our people cannot be divided. The farmer, the workingman, and the businessman must prosper together, or they go down together.

At present we are all busy and our economy is prosperous. But that prosperity can be lost if we fail to safeguard it. Right now it is threatened by inflation and by the high prices which are causing real hardship to millions of our people.

On the other hand, our prosperity can be maintained and greatly increased if we act with vision and with courage. This is essential for our own comfort and well-being. It is essential also in order that we may contribute to the economic recovery of other nations, to help secure world peace.

Consequently, it is with a sense of real urgency that I speak to you tonight about one element of our economy, one which is fundamental to all the rest. That is agriculture in this United States.

You remember what happened to the farmers shortly after the First World War? I'm sure most of you do. The farmers were hit by a disastrous slump. I ran a six-hundred-acre farm, which I was running myself with my brother. Then I went into business with a buddy, and you all know what happened to me in that slump of 1921!

In those years of farm depressions, farmers could not sell their crops for a decent price, they could not pay for the equipment they needed, they could not provide a decent living for their families. In many cases they even lost their farms and were evicted from their homes because they could not keep up the unequal struggle.

The fact that farmers were unable to recover fully from this slump helped to bring on the Great Depression of the early 1930s and carried everybody — farmers, workers, and businessmen — down together. We can't let that happen again, and if I have anything to do with it, it won't happen again!

Since the dismal period of the 1920s and the early '30s, farmers and the government have cooperated in what can truly be called the rebirth of American agriculture.

Now most of the nation's farmers are enjoying the best financial position they have ever known. Cash farm income last year reached a record high level of more than $30 billion. In 1932 it was $4,700 million. Farm mortgage debt has dropped 25 percent since 1941. Bank deposits and savings of farmers are $22 billion, the highest in our history. In 1932 you were afraid to go into a bank if you had any deposits to make, because you were afraid it would blow up in your face. In the last three years we haven't had a single bank failure in the United States.

While the present agricultural prosperity is due partly to special factors in the postwar situation, the sound farm legislation which has been adopted since 1932 provides a much better basis for sustained agricultural prosperity than we have ever had before. If you think back for a minute to 1932, you'll remember that we then had no soil conservation program, no price support program, no school lunch program, only a limited research program. In the years since that time, we have built up these and other valuable farm programs, until today there is a solid basis for further agricultural progress. But even though most of our farmers are better off than they have ever been before, farmers are concerned lest a sudden change may result in the bottom falling out of agricultural prices, as it did in 1921.

The American farmer has done a great production job during and since the war. That is the greatest agricultural production job in the history of the world. In spite of shortages of labor, machinery, fertilizer, and many other materials, he has stepped up farm output to meet our needs. This was an essential contribution to winning the war and to helping worldwide recovery after the war. Our farmers have earned the right to real protection against a postwar slump.

We need not — and we must not — allow an agricultural depression to happen. This is part of a larger problem — that of preventing general economic depressions. I believe that we should use every power and resource of the government to maintain maximum employment, production, and purchasing power throughout the whole economy. I believe that a most vital part of this effort must be directed toward meeting agricultural problems. We need action, and action now, to make sure that our farmers hold the gains they have made since 1932 and that we move forward with the job of providing future organized, sustained, realistic abundance for American agriculture.

We should also be deeply concerned about the many farm families who are not sharing fairly in the progress of American life. In far too many farm communities, housing, medical services, and educational facilities are inadequate. Some farmers are isolated by poor roads. Some still do not have electricity. Here again we need action, and action now, so that more farm areas will have better housing, adequate health services, good schools and good roads, electricity, and all the other benefits of modern living.

I believe that the federal government has a definite part to play in building for lasting agricultural prosperity and in assisting farm areas to obtain better living standards. The sound and far-reaching agricultural legislation we now have constitutes an excellent basis for continued progress. But we do need a number of extensions and improvements in our present farm programs.

First, the Congress should provide a permanent system of flexible price supports for agricultural commodities. For the benefit of farmers and the whole nation, we need price support legislation which will assure reasonable stability of farm income while encouraging desirable adjustments in production.

Wartime legislation for price support programs will expire next December. It must be replaced. Farmers right now don't know what to expect in case of crops that go beyond the end of the year, including the important winter wheat crop. I believe that the American farmer has the right to expect his government to prevent prices of farm commodities from falling to ruinous levels. I believe also that the entire nation should be protected against the wide swings in farm prices that have contributed in the past to economic insecurity for us all.

A second important program for the future of the American agriculture is that of soil conservation. Our present soil conservation program must be vigorously supported and rapidly extended.

We have been preaching conservation in this country for more than forty years, but it was not until the 1930s that we began to make important progress in conserving the soil — the most basic of all our resources. Today the soil conservation program is going strong. We have come to realize more and more the vital necessity for protecting the thin layer of topsoil which sustains our national life. Throughout the country, farmers have organized two thousand soil conservation districts to push this work forward, and the operators of nearly three million farms are cooperating today in the agricultural conservation program.

But I don't think we should be satisfied until every acre of farmland in the United States is being properly managed so that its fertility will be permanently maintained. We must not, through ignorance or misguided economy, lose any more of our vital soil resources. You know what I think? A large part of the fertile topsoil of Iowa and Nebraska and Missouri and Kansas is down at the mouth of the Mississippi River trying to make another county for Louisiana, and we mustn't let that keep up!

As a third element of major importance to agricultural prosperity, we must take steps to maintain adequate markets for farm products and to improve the methods of distributing them to consumers. The principal market for our farm products is here at home, among the American people. The best assurance of farm prosperity, therefore, is general prosperity for the whole country.

But aside from doing all it can to assure general prosperity, the federal government should take specific steps to maintain strong and steady farm markets. For example, we need to press forward with our research program to develop new uses for farm products. We must also continue to take steps, in cooperation with other governments, to encourage export markets for many of our important farm commodities.

American farmers cannot expect to be prosperous if our trade with other nations is strangled by high tariffs or other trade barriers. In this regard, the most important step we can take is to extend the Reciprocal Trade Agreements Act for three years in its present form. The bill that is now pending before the Congress has been amended to death. Just as well repeal the Reciprocal Trade Agreements and go back to Hawley-Smoot, because that's what a lot of people in the Congress would like to do.

We have a great opportunity, also, to develop programs which will help to assure stable markets for the products of our farms and at the same time will improve the health and diets of our people. The excellent school lunch program which has been worked out in recent years, for example, should be extended and strengthened.

I believe that we should also start now to develop a practical plan for safeguarding the diets of low-income families. We should have such a plan ready all the time on a standby basis, to be put into operation on short notice in case of need. We must never again allow Americans to go hungry while agricultural surpluses are going to waste.

Both farmers and consumers will be helped by continued improvements in the distribution of farm commodities. We all have the right to expect reasonable efficiency and minimum of waste in processing, transporting, and distributing farm products. And we have the right to expect a reasonable relationship between the price the farmer receives for his commodities and the price the consumer must pay for them.

I believe very strongly that the government should continue to encourage farm cooperatives. Cooperatives have proved their usefulness and their right of survival in a free enterprise system. But they are now under heavy attack. Some people, through selfishness or lack of foresight, seek to destroy cooperatives or to limit their effectiveness. We must stand firm against these attacks.

I have spoken of price supports, and soil conservation, and the marketing and distribution. The fourth major element which I believe should continue to be a part of our national agricultural program is this: the federal government should assist farmers in meeting special problems of their occupation, just as it gives assistance to other great segments of our population.

I have recommended to the Congress, for example, measures to provide better health services to farm communities, and measures to help farm families get better houses. Better roads should be provided in many agricultural areas. We should go forward with rural electrification as rapidly as possible to bring the blessings of electricity — and they are real blessings — to the farms which they have not yet reached.

All the measures I have been discussing tonight are sound, practical steps needed to assure the future welfare of American agriculture. They represent no great change in our national policy but instead are designed to improve and build upon the sound foundation we already have.

A number of measures I have been talking about need to be enacted into law. Since the beginning of the 80th Congress, in January 1947, I have been recommending action on this necessary legislation. The secretary of agriculture has presented the program in detail to the Congress on a number of occasions. The Congress has considered it and studied it and weighed it and pondered it. But the Congress has not acted upon it.

We must not give up hope, however. There is still time for Congress to act. I am sure that American farmers join me in the wish that the Congress will not leave Washington without passing the farm legislation we need.

Here in Nebraska a few weeks ago there was a primary election. A lot of prominent politicians were interested in the outcome of that election. It happens that Nebraska is justly famous as a great independent farm state, in the heart of the agricultural region of the Middle West — the breadbasket of the nation and the world. So these prominent politicians got the idea that they should come out here to Nebraska and make farm speeches. And that's what they did.

They came and said they were for the farmers; they said they were for a farm program; they said they were for the enactment of legislation needed for a farm program. Now, I must confess to you that these same politicians have great influence with the present Congress. So I think we might properly ask, "Why doesn't Congress act?"

Now, I believe that is a fair question. I believe the time has passed when a man can be *for* a farm program in the West and against a farm program when he is back East. If everybody is in favor of a farm program, now is the time for Congress to act upon it.

We have it within our power to bring sound and lasting prosperity to our farms and to improve the standard of living here in our own country and in other countries. This is the course we must follow to build for our future and to make our full contribution to the peace and freedom of the world.

NOTE: The president's opening words "Mr. Chairmen" referred to Edward D. McKim and Robert A. Drum, who served as cochairmen of the reunion. The address was carried on a nationwide radio broadcast.

★ ★ ★ ★ ★ ★ ★ ★ ★ ★ ★ ★ ★ ★ ★ ★

JUNE 10

Address before the Washington State Press Club
Memorial High School Stadium, Seattle (2:30 P.M.)

Mr. Chairman, Mr. Mayor, Governor Wallgren:

I have a distinguished lady to introduce at this time, the first lady of the great state of Washington, Mrs. Wallgren.

I am very happy to be with you today. The trip west has been an education to me, and I hope it will be an education to the country before I get through.

I received a very sad message from Washington this morning. I was notified about 5:00 this morning that Secretary of Labor Lewis Schwellenbach had passed away last night. Senator Schwellenbach — I always called him Senator Schwellenbach — he introduced me here in this city the first time I was ever here. He and I served in the Senate. He was an able senator, a just judge, and a very great secretary of labor. The country has lost a real public servant, and I have lost a close personal friend — and I am sorry.

Cheering throngs turned out for HST in Seattle. "I think I have seen more people on this trip," Truman said of his western tour, "than any other president ever saw on one trip." (Chicago Sun-Times)

Yesterday, I visited Grand Coulee Dam for the third time. The sight of that great project moved me deeply, as it has moved me in the past. For Grand Coulee has significance far beyond the direct contribution it makes to the prosperity of the Pacific Northwest, vital as that is. To me, that magnificent structure stands for many things for which I stand, and for which I have always voted in the Senate.

It stands for the wise use of the natural resources with which God has endowed us for the benefit of all the people. It stands for the use of water for two purposes essential to the growth of the West — irrigation and power. It stands for the industrial development of the West, which is so vital for the growth of this whole nation. It stands for the courage and determination of farsighted citizens, who kept up the fight for the construction of this dam until that fight was won. It stands for the use of the powers of the federal government to promote the welfare of its citizens. And, finally, it stands for the great heart and the great vision of one who did so much to make it possible — Franklin D. Roosevelt.

When I saw Grand Coulee Dam yesterday, it was pounded by the waters of the worst flood that has visited the Columbia River in fifty-four years. Mr. Banks, who is in charge out there, told me that a million acre-feet of water per twenty-four hours are going over that dam. That is almost incomprehensible. This flood has taken precious human lives. It has done tremendous damage to towns and farms. I cannot express too strongly the concern that this disaster has brought to me. But it is an experience from which we can learn a lesson — or rather get added proof for a lesson that many of us just learned a long time ago.

The federal government must go forward vigorously with projects to control the waters of our rivers and direct them to useful purposes. The waters of the Columbia River can be controlled. The shock of this tragedy should reinforce our determination to build the dams and other structures needed to bring about such control. Nothing can ever completely repair the damage caused by this flood or replace the lives that have been lost. But we can do something to see that it does not happen again.

We know what must be done to achieve this. We have already proved it in the Tennessee Valley. The Tennessee River used to flood every year or so. But that doesn't happen anymore. The waters have been checked by dams. Now they are used for electric power and for navigation and recreation. Now those waters that used to rush down to the sea in floods are held and put to work.

Every year in the Tennessee Valley, millions of dollars — and probably many human lives as well — are saved because the floods have been stopped. And they can be stopped on the Columbia too.

What we have done in the Tennessee Valley we can do elsewhere. We have already been moving in that direction in other great river basins — the Missouri, the Colorado, the Central Valley of California, and the Columbia. Our purpose is the same in all of them — to conserve the use of water instead of wasting it. But to achieve that simple purpose, we must follow a unified development of all the resources of each valley. And that is no easy job, for a number of reasons. Let me use the Columbia River Basin as an example.

The Columbia and its tributaries comprise a mighty river system draining parts of seven states and Canada. It discharges the second-largest flow of water of any river in the United States. To harness this vast flow will take many dams and many years of effort.

Furthermore, the Columbia Basin is rich in other resources besides water. It has fertile lands, vast bodies of timber, valuable minerals, and a multi-million-dollar fishing industry.

We cannot plan in terms of water alone. The water and the land must be considered together. They must be studied in relation to the fisheries and the forests. Hydroelectric power must be considered in relation to the processing of minerals. All natural resources must be related to the industrial development of this region. There must be, in short, a great vision of what the resources of a region can achieve if they are wisely conserved and developed together. And we must have the faith and the courage to carry out that vision.

It will take the toughest kind of fight to put over these great projects for western development. For there are people in this country and in the Congress who will not support the development of western resources. A few of them, unfortunately, hold influential positions. They are opposed or indifferent to the development of these western regions for the benefit of the people here. They still seem to look on the West as some sort of wilderness in which the nation should invest as little as possible.

I think the record is conclusive on this point. It was only fifteen years ago that the tremendous waters of the great Columbia River rushed unused to the sea. At the same time, good farmlands in the Columbia Basin lay barren and dry. Industries which needed huge volumes of low-cost power stayed elsewhere. The same story was true throughout the West. In those days, too many of the West's raw products were shipped east to be processed; and the people here got neither the jobs nor the profits involved in their manufacture into finished goods.

Prior to 1933 the Reclamation Act had been on the books for thirty years. In all that time, water for reclamation had been extended to less than three million acres throughout the West; and the hydroelectric power capacity installed on these projects was only thirty-five thousand kilowatts. Compare that with the present situation. The Grand Coulee project alone will produce ninety-two million kilowatts of power, and water for nearly a million acres of land. And there are projects on a similar scale under way all through the West.

It is easy to accept conditions as they are today and to forget the bitter struggles we went through to bring about this progress. But I am sure most of you can recall those days. When the Bonneville and Grand Coulee projects were before the Congress, they were bitterly opposed by the private power lobby. And that lobby is just as busy today as it was in that day. The lobby pointed out that there wasn't much industry in the Northwest. They claimed that these projects would turn out to be "white elephants" because there would be no use for their power. And a lot of people believed them.

But the projects were put through, and the cries of the private power lobby were proved to be absurd. The low-cost power produced at Bonneville and Grand Coulee attracted new industries to the Northwest at a rapid rate. During the war this power proved of tremendous importance. I am sure that Bonneville and Grand Coulee speeded up the victory to such an extent that they more than paid for themselves in money and men during the war.

Since the war, the growth of the Northwest has continued. The demand for power, instead of decreasing with the decline of war production, has greatly increased. I wish those congressmen — and there are a lot of them — who are still listening to the private power lobby would look at these projects now. I wish they could have been with me yesterday. These projects are turning out every last kilowatt of power they can, and new generators are being installed as fast as they can be obtained — or as fast as Congress will let us obtain them.

Moreover, the rapid industrial development of the Pacific Northwest is going to require a great deal more power in the years ahead. Let's look at some of the facts about this industrial development. In less than a decade the power from the Bonneville and Grand Coulee projects had led to the establishment in the Northwest of electric-process industries turning out $140 million worth of products each year. And those unbelievers said it couldn't be done. Many other new industries have sprung up in the Northwest. The indirect effects of industrial growth here have been felt across the nation in higher employment, higher income, and greater wealth.

For example, the new aluminum rolling mill at Spokane is selling its products to six hundred plants throughout the nation, which employ 350,000 workers. This shows that industrial development here in the West does not detract from the prosperity of any other region. Instead, it adds to the prosperity of the whole nation. The United States is still growing, and growing fast. The growth of the West means a better life for people here, and better markets and sources of supply for the rest of the country as well.

You might think that the private power interests and others who have fought against the development of the West would have learned by now that western growth means increased national prosperity. But they still haven't learned. Again the record is clear.

Last year, I asked the Congress, in my annual budget message for an appropriation of $146 million to carry forward the reclamation program for the development of water resources. There was a powerful move in the Congress to cut this back to less than $50 million. Even in the face of protests from all the western states, the House of Representatives voted to cut my figure by more than half. And this year the Congress doesn't seem to be quite so interested in holding back the development of the West. But I have a suspicion that this might have something to do with the fact that this is 1948. I do not believe that the people of the West will go along with a system that appropriates enough money for western development only one year in four. And even this year, the appropriation of adequate funds is in doubt.

Some of the people who oppose western development represent selfish interests who are more concerned with present profits than with future growth. They refuse to admit that funds spent for reclamation projects and power plants and navigation locks and fish ladders are investments which pay huge dividends as the years go by to the people of the United States.

This administration is determined that it will continue to move ahead with a constructive, practical program against the delaying tactics of ignorance and selfishness. It will fight in the future with the same vigor as it has fought in the past.

The private power lobbyists are still fighting. Where they can't block the production of public power, they're trying to block its distribution at low cost. For example, down in California, Shasta Dam has been completed and has begun to turn out power. If that power is to be used for the people's benefit, it must be moved over the transmission lines to the areas where it's needed. But the Congress has blocked the building of the necessary transmission lines year after year. This has been at the expense of the public and to the benefit of a private company. We can't stand for that. And if you people out here stand for it, it is your own loss. I am fighting for you. Now you do some fighting for yourselves. This is the same company which has so little faith in the future of the West that it failed this spring to be ready to furnish vitally needed power. As a result, the whole of northern California has to resort to a "brown-out." Those people are just like the Aluminum Company of America, where not so long ago old man Davis came down and told me that 300 million pounds of aluminum was all the country would ever use, and that was enough. You have got 3,500 million capacity now, and we are short!

There is no reason why the public should be forced to suffer in this manner. Utility companies must not be allowed to block publicly owned transmission lines which will bring public power to the people at low cost.

As more and more public power becomes available from the great dams all through the West, we can see the time when all the great systems will connect together. From the Colorado through the Central Valley up to the Columbia Basin, there should be a vast network of high-voltage transmission lines. I suppose when that time comes, we'll still have to battle with the men of little faith! I am sure of it. You had better wake up.

The fight over whether or not publicly produced power shall be used for the public benefit is only a part of the larger battle concerning the development of the basic resources of our great river valleys. One important lesson we have learned from the Tennessee Valley experience is that the resources of a watershed area must be developed jointly and in relation to each other if they are to contribute everything possible to the development of the region. A second great lesson we have learned from the Tennessee Valley is that the local, state, and federal governments must work together in regional development if that development is to be in fact for the benefit of the people. I have urged time and time again that the experience of the TVA shows the way in which we should move in other great river basins.

We are only a small distance along the road we want to travel. Water that can be used for power, for irrigation, for navigation, is going to waste all over the country. Millions of acres of land that are now dry or swampy can be put to work in productive agriculture. Soil, water, and forest conservation is just beginning to be understood and put into practice on the scale needed.

In the Columbia River Basin, Bonneville and Grand Coulee mark a fine beginning. But we must have more dams in that mighty stream if it is to be effectively harnessed for useful purposes. I believe the present flood shows that we should try to make progress even faster than we had planned — not slower. Last year the Congress threw us backward when it cut the appropriations for this work. The cuts that are threatened this year will throw us back again if they are made. Such cuts as this are the worst kind of false economy. You know what they are doing with these appropriations now? They are tying them up in such a way that even if we get them, we can't use them to the best advantage and the best interests of the public.

All of us should take to heart the tragic events that have happened here in the Northwest in the last few weeks. If we don't conserve our resources wisely, we shall pay a terrible price. We cannot afford that price if we are to remain strong and to enjoy a better life in the years to come. Let us keep before us the goal of using all our natural resources fully, for the benefit of our children as well as for ourselves.

But we will have to battle every step of the way. There will still be men of little faith who are afraid to trust to the people the development of the resources of the nation. I believe we have the courage and the will and the vision to carry the program through in spite of these men. I believe the people here in the Northwest, and in every other part of the country, understand the issue clearly and will choose the path of growth and progress.

We know what must be done and we know how it can be done. But in order to get it done, you must make your voices so plainly heard in the Congress that there will be no mistaking your will and your faith in the future of this great nation.

NOTE: In his opening words the president referred to William Devin, mayor of Seattle, and Mon C. Wallgren, governor of Washington. Later he referred to Frank A. Banks, district manager of the Grand Coulee Dam. Dudley M. Brown served as president of the Washington State Press Club, and Emil G. Sick served as general chairman. The address was carried on a nationwide radio broadcast.

★ ★ ★ ★ ★ ★ ★ ★ ★ ★ ★ ★ ★ ★ ★ ★ ★ ★

Rear Platform Remarks

Eugene, Oregon (6:25 P.M.)

It certainly is fine to see all of you here today. The last time I was here, it was 7:00 in the morning. There weren't quite so many of you up that time. I was going from San Francisco to Portland in 1944, in the campaign of 1944. It was my duty to start that campaign in Los Angeles, California, which I did, and I came to San Francisco, and then to Eugene, then to Portland, then to Seattle, and all the way across the country. Thirteen thousand miles I went on that tour. I won't go quite so far on this one, but I may take one later on that will take a little more time.

I came out here this time to discuss with you certain things in which you are interested, and I think I have been rather successful in making you see that there are things in which you are interested, and which I am interested in also, but I fear very much that the Congress is not so interested as we are in those things. I want you to find that out for yourselves. I understand that this is the seat of the University of Oregon, and that more than half the students are GIs. That is a wonderful thing. Those GIs found out that they needed an education, and they found out that they could get it, and they found out that those of us who had been in the Congress were thinking about them and trying to make arrangements so that they could get an education. You know that education is one thing that can't be taken away from you. Nobody can rob you of your education, because that is in your head — that is, if you have any head and are capable of holding it. Most of us are capable of holding an education, if we try to get it.

I sent my daughter to George Washington University, and it took her four long years to get a degree, and I got one the same night for nothing! I have never been to the University of California either, but I am going down there tomorrow to get another degree, and I didn't do anything for it, only I am going to make a graduation speech there and tell them all about foreign affairs and the foreign policy of the United States of America. I hope you will all listen to that because it is only a repeat of what I have said at least a hundred times. It is the foreign policy of the United States that I am going to discuss tomorrow at the University of California, and you are all interested in it, because if we carry out that foreign policy, we will have peace in the world. And that's what everybody wants. I want peace in the world just as badly as anybody in the world.

I went to Potsdam in 1945 with that in view. I went there with the kindliest feelings in the world toward Russia, and we made certain agreements, specific agreements. I got very well acquainted with Joe Stalin, and I like old Joe! He is a decent fellow. But Joe is a prisoner of the politburo. He can't do what he wants to. He makes agreements, and if he could, he would keep them; but the people who run the government are very specific in saying that he can't keep them.

Now, sometime or other that great country and this great country are going to understand that their mutual interests mean the welfare and peace of the world as a whole. I am going to tell you about that tomorrow at the University of California.

★ Oakridge, Oregon (7:40 P.M.)

Mr. Mayor and citizens of Oakridge City, Oregon:

The mayor tells me that he is a blacksmith by trade. You know, that is what makes this country great. Anybody can be mayor, congressman, senator, president, you see. And that is the reason I am happy to be a citizen of the great state of Missouri. You know, all of you had to come through Missouri — your ancestors did — before you could get to Oregon. You all came down the Oregon Trail, which originated in Independence, Missouri.

I am most happy that the train stopped here tonight, and I am most happy to have a chance to say a word to you. Thank you a lot. I certainly appreciate this welcome.

★ Klamath Falls, Oregon (10:55 P.M.)

Thank you very much, Mr. Mayor. I have had a most enjoyable visit on this west coast. I don't think I ever received a more cordial welcome than I have received in Washington and Oregon. They have been exceedingly kind to me, and I can't tell you how much I appreciate it.

The president, you know, has to receive all the criticism that it's possible for a man to receive and still survive. So when he sees smiling faces such as yours, and such as I have seen along the railroad today, it is a compensation for what he had to go through with being president.

The president's job is a remarkable one. He is the chief executive of the greatest nation in the world. He has certain responsibilities which he cannot forgo. He must stay at the table and work day in and day out, and year in and year out, hoping that he will accomplish something that will be for the benefit of all the people of the nation. And if he can do that, then he is satisfied. Sometimes he thinks he has succeeded. More often he is afraid he has not, especially if he believes the columnists that write in some of the newspapers.

Since I have been in the White House, since April 12, on that sad day when President Roosevelt died, I have had a varied experience. Two wars have ended in that time, and we have been endeavoring ever since those two wars ended to get a peace. That is my one ambition, to get peace in the world.

I had hoped in September 1945, when the Japanese surrender terms were signed, that by this time we would have peace in the world. We are going to get peace in the world, because that is what we must have. The United Nations is the vehicle through which we will get peace in the world. And when that peace comes, I am just as sure as I stand here that the atomic age is going to be the greatest age in history. I have said many times that I wish I were eighteen years old, or younger, so I could go along with the world that is to come.

You know, way back in 1845, there was a certain prime minister of Great Britain who said that he was glad he was retiring as prime minister of Great Britain, because he thought the empire was going to break up. Well, Britain accomplished its greatest period after 1845.

We had a patent commissioner along in 1843 who went down and told the Senate Appropriations Committee that the Patent Office ought to be abolished because there was nothing new to invent. That was in 1843. What great changes — this business I am talking over right now, this radio — the automobile, electric light, and everything else that we use and think we cannot get along today without, they were all invented and patented since 1843. Suppose the Senate Appropriations Committee had followed the advice of the old patent commissioner? We would be in exactly the same position that we will be if we listen to the gloom artists today.

I am not gloomy. I think we are facing the greatest age in history. And I think all you young people are going to have a glorious future. I think this great nation has only begun to be great, because in 1920 Almighty God expected us to assume the leadership of the world, which we refused to assume, and we had another war.

We are faced now with that same situation. We must assume that leadership, and I am trying my best to see that this nation does assume that leadership. And if you support me in it, we are going to assume it.

NOTE: In the course of his remarks on June 11 the president referred to Lorenz F. Gerspach, mayor of Oakridge, and Ed Ostendorn, mayor of Klamath Falls.

★ ★ ★ ★ ★ ★ ★ ★ ★ ★ ★ ★ ★ ★ ★ ★ ★

JUNE 12

Commencement Address

Memorial Stadium, University of California, Berkeley (4 P.M.)

President Sproul, distinguished guests, ladies and gentlemen:

I deeply appreciate the privilege you have given me of taking part in these exercises at this great university. I regret that I could not arrange my schedule to permit me to be here next week at the time for which you first invited me. Under these circumstances, I am pleased that an adjustment could be made on the part of the university so as to make it possible for me to be here today.

Three years ago this month, across the bay in San Francisco, I witnessed the signing of the Charter of the United Nations. That charter represents man's hope for a world order based upon law, and for lasting peace based on justice. Today I have come back to the shores of San Francisco Bay to discuss with you recent world events and, in particular, to appraise the progress we are making toward world peace.

Many students here today and in colleges across the country are veterans. They fought for peace with freedom and justice. They, above all, have reason to expect a plain statement of the progress we are making in that direction.

The American people know from experience that our daily lives are affected not only by what happens in this country but also by events abroad. Most American families bear the scars and memories of a war which began thousands of miles from this nation. Every American wants to be sure that this country is doing everything in its power to build a lasting peace and a just peace. We believe that such a peace can be achieved by the nations of the world.

Anyone can talk peace. But only the work that is done for peace really counts. I propose to describe the specific steps the United States has taken to obtain peace in the world. I propose also to discuss what further measures we must take, and what measures others must take, if our hopes for peace are to be fulfilled.

The United States has consistently done its part in meeting the requirements for a peaceful world. We fought through World War II with only one purpose: to destroy the tyrants who tried to impose their rule on the world and enslave the people. We sought no territories; we asked for only token reparations. At the end of the war, we quickly dismantled the greatest military machine ever built by any nation. We withdrew and demobilized the American armies that had swept across Europe and the Pacific, leaving only minimum occupation forces in Germany, Austria, Japan, and Korea. The nations which our army had helped to liberate were left free to work out their postwar problems without interference from us. That was not the course of a nation that sought to impose its will upon others. It was not the course of an aggressor.

Long before the fighting had ended, our government began planning for a world organization which could provide security for all nations. At Dumbarton Oaks, at Yalta, at San Francisco, the United States led the way in preparing for a strong and useful United Nations. In the past three years we have taken a leading part in establishing the United Nations and the related agencies — such as the World Bank and the Food and Agriculture Organization —which are fundamental to world peace and prosperity.

No action by the United States has revealed more clearly our sincere desire for peace than our proposal in the United Nations for the international control of atomic energy. In a step without precedent, we have voluntarily offered to share with others the secrets of atomic power. We ask only for conditions that will guarantee its use for the benefit of humanity — and not for the destruction of humanity.

To assist world economic recovery, we have contributed nearly $20 billion in loans and grants to other nations. American dollars have been invested generously in the cause of peace because we know what peace is worth.

This is a record of action in behalf of peace without parallel in history.

Many other nations have joined wholeheartedly with us in our work for peace. They share our desire for international control of atomic energy, for the early conclusion of peace treaties, for world economic recovery, and for the effective development of the United Nations.

Why then, after such great exertions and huge expenditures, do we live today in a twilight period, between war so dearly won and a peace that still eludes our grasp? The answer is not hard to find. It lies largely in the attitude of one nation — the Soviet Union.

Long before the war, the United States established normal diplomatic and commercial relations with the Soviet Union. In doing so, we demonstrated our belief that it was possible to get along with a nation whose economic and political system differs sharply from ours.

During the war, we worked with the Soviet Union wholeheartedly in defeating the common enemy. In every way we could, we tried to convince the Soviet government that it was possible and necessary for allied unity to continue the great task of establishing the peace. We hoped that the Soviet Union, secure in her own strength and doubly secure in respect of her allies, would accept full partnership in a peaceful world community.

The record, however, is clear for all to read. The Soviet government has rejected the invitation to participate, freely and on equal terms, in a great cooperative program for reconstruction of Europe. It has constantly maneuvered for delay and for propaganda effect in every international conference. It has used its veto excessively and unreasonably in the Security Council of the United Nations. It has boycotted the "Little Assembly" and several special United Nations commissions. It has used indirect aggression against a number of nations in Eastern Europe and extreme pressure against others in the Middle East. It has intervened in the internal affairs of many other countries by means of Communist parties directed from Moscow. The refusal of the Soviet Union to work with its wartime allies for world recovery and world peace is the most bitter disappointment of our time.

The great issues of world peace and world recovery are sometimes portrayed as disputes solely between the United States and the Soviet Union. This is not the case. The fact is that not a single one of the major unsettled questions of the postwar world is primarily a disagreement between this country and the Soviet Union. We are not engaged in a struggle with the Soviet Union for any territory or for any economic gain. We have no hostile or aggressive designs against the Soviet Union or any other country. We are not waging a "cold war."

The cleavage that exists is not between the Soviet Union and the United States. It is between the Soviet Union and the rest of the world. The great questions at stake today affect not only the United States and the Soviet Union; they affect all nations. Whether it be the control of atomic energy, aggression against small nations, the German or the Austrian peace settlements, or any of the other questions, the majority of nations concerned have found a common basis for action. But in every case the majority agreement has been rejected, denounced, and openly attacked by the Soviet Union and her satellites whose policy she controls.

Let me repeat: the division has been not between the United States and the Soviet Union but between the Soviet Union and the free nations of the world.

The United States is strongly devoted to the principle of discussion and negotiation in settling international differences. We do not believe in settling differences by force. There are certain types of disputes in international affairs which can and must be settled by negotiation and agreement.

But there are others which are not susceptible to negotiation. There is nothing to negotiate when one nation disregards the principles of international conduct to which all the members of the United Nations have subscribed. There is nothing to negotiate when one nation habitually uses coercion and open aggression in international affairs.

What the world needs in order to regain a sense of security is an end to Soviet obstruction and aggression. I will give you two clear illustrations of what I have in mind.

The situation in Greece has caused a great deal of uneasiness throughout the world. It has been the subject of a series of investigations on the part of commissions of the United Nations. The facts have been established over and over again by these investigations. They are clear beyond dispute. Some twenty thousand Greek guerrillas have been able to keep Greece in a state of unrest and to disrupt Greek recovery, primarily because of the aid and comfort they have been receiving from the neighboring countries of Bulgaria, Yugoslavia, and Albania.

Last October the United Nations General Assembly adopted a resolution calling upon Bulgaria, Yugoslavia, and Albania to stop their illegal aid and comfort to the Greek rebels. This resolution was agreed to by more than two-thirds of the membership of the United Nations. But it has been boycotted by Russia.

The situation in Greece requires no special negotiation or discussion or conference. On its own initiative the Soviet government can cease its boycott of the United Nations recommendation. It can join with other nations in stopping illegal foreign support of the Greek guerrillas so that Greece may have an opportunity for peaceful reconstruction. If the Soviet Union genuinely desires to make a contribution to the peace and recovery of the world, it can prove it in Greece.

The situation in Korea is also disturbing. There the Soviet government has defied the clearly expressed will of an overwhelming majority of the United Nations, by boycotting the United Nations Temporary Commission on Korea. This commission was created last fall by the General Assembly to help set up a Korean national government based on free and democratic elections. The Soviet boycott has prevented the residents of the northern zone of Korea from electing representatives to establish a unified national government for Korea.

The situation in Korea requires no special negotiation or discussion or conference. On its own initiative the Soviet Union can abandon its boycott of the United Nations commission. It can permit the people of North Korea to work with their compatriots in the south in creating an independent and democratic nation. If the Soviet Union genuinely desires to make a contribution to peace and recovery in the world, it can prove it in Korea.

In these questions, as in all others, there are practical ways for the Soviet Union to show its good faith by proper action. The United States will always respond to an honest move by any nation to further the principles and purposes of the Charter of the United Nations. But no nation has the right to exact a price for good behavior.

What is needed is a will for peace. What is needed is the abandonment of the absurd idea that the capitalistic nations will collapse and that the instability in international affairs will hasten their collapse, leaving the world free for communism. It is possible for different economic systems to live side by side in peace, one with the other, provided one of these systems is not determined to destroy the other by force.

I have said before and I repeat now: the door is always open for honest negotiations looking toward genuine settlements.

The door is not open, however, for deals between great powers to the detriment of other nations or at the expense of principle. We refuse to play fast and loose with man's hope for peace. That hope is too sacred to be trifled with for propaganda purposes, or selfish advantage, by any individual or nation. We are interested in peace — not in propaganda. We shall judge the policy of every nation by whether it advances or obstructs world progress toward peace, and we wish our own policy to be judged by the same standard.

I stated our American policy for peace at the end of the war. It has been restated many times, but I shall repeat the essential elements of our policy again so that there can be no misunderstanding anywhere by anyone.

We seek no territorial expansion or selfish advantage.
We have no plans for aggression against any other state, large or small.
We have no objective which need clash with the peaceful aims of any other nation.

The United States has been conscientious and consistent in its devotion to those principles. We have sought to assist free nations in creating economic conditions under which free institutions can survive and flourish. We have sought through the United Nations the development of a world order in which each nation feels secure under law and can make its contribution to world civilization in accordance with its own means and national tradition. We have sought to help free nations protect themselves against aggression. We know that peace through weakness has proved to be a dangerous illusion. We are determined, therefore, to keep strong for the sake of peace.

This course is not an easy one. But it is the practical, realistic path to peace. It has required, and will continue to require, hard work and some sacrifice by the people of the United States. But from many quarters there is tangible evidence that it is succeeding.

This is the course we must follow. I do not propose that we shall be turned aside by those who want to see us fail. Our policy will continue to be a policy of recovery, reconstruction, prosperity — and peace with freedom and justice. In its furtherance, we gladly join with all those of like purpose.

The only expansion we are interested in is the expansion of human freedom and the wider enjoyment of the good things of the earth in all countries. The only prize we covet is the respect and goodwill of our fellow members of family of nations. The only realm in which we aspire to eminence exists in the minds of men, where authority is exercised through the qualities of sincerity, compassion, and right conduct. Abiding devotion to these ideals, and profound faith in their ultimate triumph, sustain and guide the American people in the service of the most compelling cause of our time — the crusade for peace.

I believe the men and women of every part of the globe intensely desire peace and freedom. I believe good people everywhere will not permit their rulers, no matter how powerful they may have made themselves, to lead them to destruction. America has faith in people. It knows that rulers rise and fall but that people live on. The American people, from the mighty rostrum of the United Nations, call out to all peoples of the world to join with them to preserve the peace.

NOTE: The president's opening words "President Sproul" referred to Dr. Robert G. Sproul, president of the university. The address was carried on a nationwide radio broadcast.

★ ★ ★ ★ ★ ★ ★ ★ ★ ★ ★ ★ ★ ★ ★ ★

JUNE 14

Address before the Greater Los Angeles Press Club
Ambassador Hotel, Los Angeles (1:30 P.M.)

Mr. President, Governor Knight, Mr. Mayor, distinguished guests, and members of the press club:

This has been a most rousing welcome in this great city in sunny California. The mayor of Omaha told me that the greatest crowd that has even been on the streets of Omaha was there to see me in that great city. At Butte, Montana, there were more people in the arena than live in Butte. I think they must have come from miles around in order to see what I look like and hear what I had to say. At Spokane, Washington, early in the morning, there were about two acres of people in the town, down in the park and in the center of the town. In Seattle, the greatest reception, they said, that has been given to anybody in that great city. San Francisco, the same way. And here you top them all.

The reason I make that reference [is that] it was said over the radio the other night by a member of the Senate that I was stopping at the whistle-stops, misinforming the people about the situation. Los Angeles is the biggest whistle-stop.

I have been trying to speak on the issues on this trip before the country. That is my privilege as president of the United States. I have a right and a duty to inform the people what I believe is good for the country. And I took this opportunity, before Congress adjourned, because I think there are some things the Congress has not done that they should have done, and I want to give them the opportunity to find out what the people think of those things that they have not done. Therefore, I took this trip before the Congress adjourned, in order that they may have an opportunity to act. I sincerely hope that they will take advantage of that opportunity. They still have time. And if they haven't time, they ought to take it.

And I wanted the record to be entirely clear. Congress should pass laws for the benefit of all the people, in my opinion, and they should pass those laws to meet the situations with which we are faced, and we are faced with some very serious situations.

The one I think that is most important and is closest to everyone is prices. Prices have been on the skyrocket ever since July 1946, when the price control law was repealed, by furnishing me with an impossible law, which I had to sign because I had vetoed one just as bad on the 30th of June. I had to take the law of July 31 or have none. And I said at that time that it was worse than none, and it turned out to be just that.

Now, on the price index — which is made by the Bureau of Labor Statistics and on which everyone in the country relies for the situation in the price setup — at the time that those price controls were released, it was in the neighborhood of 130 or 133. Immediately after those price controls were released, that price index went up 20 points, and it has been steadily climbing ever since. It now stands in the neighborhood of 172 and a fraction. That means that costs of everything which you have to buy — food, clothing, everything which you have to buy — has gone up almost 50 percent. That means that the dollar that was worth a dollar at 133 is worth about 66 ⅔ cents at the present time.

Now, in September 1945, in my message to the Congress, which stated the twenty-one points on which I proposed to stand as president, I asked for an extension of the price control law, which expired June 30, 1946. In the Message on the State of the Union in January 1946, I made the same request. I got nothing. And I got a law that was no good, that didn't work. I called a special session of the Congress in November 1947. In the meantime, in the Message on the State of the Union, I had told the Congress what the state of the price situation was at that time, but in November 1947, when the special session was called, I set out a ten-point program, which I asked the Congress to give me to meet the situation with which we were faced in regard to prices and commodities. You know, the object of the price control law in wartime was to protect the consumer. It was a consumer's price control law.

This 80th Congress has said that prices would adjust themselves. Well, the prices have adjusted themselves. Well, the prices have adjusted themselves and are adjusting themselves. They have almost gone off the graph adjusting themselves in favor of the man who controls the goods, and the consumer pays through the nose.

Now that situation has not been met. We should have a standby price control law to be put into effect when it is necessary, and it is necessary, right now. And we should have an allocation law which would allow the allocation of scarce materials into channels where they will do the most good. Nothing has been done about that situation. I still hope the Congress will act.

Now, the next thing in which you are vitally interested down here, and every great city in the country is vitally interested, is housing. Housing. Four years ago while I was in the Senate, the Senate passed a bill called the Wagner-Ellender-Taft Housing Bill. That bill died in the House. Efforts have continually been made ever since that time to pass that bill. And the fundamental thing in that bill is a federal low-cost housing program — that is, low-cost rental program. Had that bill been passed four years ago, or two years ago, or one year ago, we would be beginning to get some benefit from it now.

This city, I think, understands the housing shortage better than the Congress does. When I was here during wartime, you had an immense housing shortage. The mayor tells me that the situation has not improved, because every GI who was trained in this part of the world wants to come back here to live.

That Taft-Ellender-Wagner bill — you see, they reversed it in this 80th Congress — has passed the Senate and is now pending in the House. It would still be helpful if the House would pass that bill. The chairman of the Committee on Banking and Currency in the House has been sitting on the bill. But the other day he got the surprise of his lifetime. The committee took the bit in the teeth, and 11 Democrats and 3 Republicans voted that bill out to the calendar of the House by a vote of 14 to 13. Eleven Democrats and 3 Republicans voted that bill out.

Now it is necessary under the House rules that a rule be made so that that bill may be debated on the floor of the House and passed. The Rules Committee now can roost on that bill until the Congress adjourns, unless the people of the United States wake up and do something about it and force action.

The chairman of the Rules Committee is a little bit tougher than the chairman of the Banking and Currency Committee, so I doubt very much whether we will get action. But the Congress ought to stay in session until we get action on the housing bill. It is vitally important. It is vitally important for the welfare of this country that we have proper housing at a cost at which men and women can afford to live in the houses, at a cost which will not take everything that these GIs have, at a cost which will be easy on the people who have to pay the bills.

I think the Wagner-Taft-Ellender bill, in all probability, can help to meet that situation. I sincerely hope something will be done about it.

Now I have another subject on which — in which — you are vitally interested and which I have been discussing on this trip, and that is the labor situation. The Republican platform of 1944, in bold, broad type, made the statement that they would build up a real Labor Department, that they would strengthen the Labor Department. You know what they have done to the Labor Department? They have practically abolished the Labor Department. They have practically put the Labor Department out of business, not by proper legislation but by choking it to death with appropriations that are not sufficient.

The last great contribution that this 80th Congress made to the Labor Department was to choke off the Bureau of Labor Statistics, so that it is impossible for them to act, and every business, every branch of the government, is dependent upon the Bureau of Labor Statistics to find out just exactly what is happening to prices and in the labor market and everything else that goes on where statistics are needed. You see, they were not satisfied with taking the lid off the prices and letting them go to a mile-a-minute rate. They wanted to jerk the speedometer out of the car so you can't see how fast you are going into inflation.

Well, the last great effort that has been made on the Labor Department was to take the U.S. Employment Services out of the Labor Department. They have already taken the Conciliation Service out of the Labor Department, and I am saying to you that I think the Labor Department is one of the most important and necessary departments of this government, and I think the

Congress ought to study this situation and take the necessary action to restore the Labor Department to the department which I had built it up to in the first two years I took over.

The Labor Department suffered during the war. It necessarily had to suffer during the war on account of the special agencies which had to work during the war. I have been trying to restore that Labor Department to its prewar height. That is what ought to happen. I think the Congress ought to take some action on that before they quit.

Now, the Republican platform was very much interested in Social Security. I have been asking the Congress to broaden the base of Social Security so more people could benefit from the Social Security Act, so that more people could get the benefit of employment insurance and help to pay it while they worked, so that they will be contributing to their support when they are out of work and will not have to go on relief.

Well, you know how the Congress has broadened the base of Social Security? They have just taken 750,000 people off Social Security and sent me a bill to that effect and tied a rider onto it, increasing old-age assistance, hoping that I would take that bait and let them get away with wrecking Social Security.

I didn't do it. I vetoed that bill this morning, and I told the Congress that if it would pass the Congress in the proper form, I would be happy to sign it. And they have plenty of time to pass it in the proper form. Don't think they haven't.

Now, I have had a health program. I sent the Congress a special message on health — on health and health insurance — and it had plenty of time to hold hearings on that, to debate it, to go into it, and they have done nothing about it. Now the health of this nation is the foundation on which the nation is built. I have made a personal study of that situation. We have got a health and accident situation in this country that is the most disgraceful of any country in the world. There are only two classes of people that can get the proper medical care nowadays, and that is the indigent and the very rich. The ordinary fellow who gets from $2,400 to $5,000 a year and has to raise a family and keep up a home can't afford to have his family get sick, because he can't afford medical care at the prices he has to be served at now. Something ought to be done about that. A healthy nation is a great nation, and unless we maintain the health of this nation, we will not have a great nation.

I am interested also in those people who are disabled in industry. I am just as anxious to see those people restored to working ability as I am to see these crippled GIs properly taken care of. We have done a magnificent job with the GIs. We can do the same thing for those people who are crippled in industry.

In Seattle the other day I was in an institution that was just starting to rehabilitate men and women who are injured in industry. Do you know that there are in the neighborhood of twenty-six million people in this country who have been injured and who are permanently disabled or temporarily disabled, and that the vast majority of those people could be rehabilitated and be back on a self-supporting basis if the situation was properly approached? That is appalling, and the vast majority of those people are injured in automobile accidents. The most terrible weapon that was ever invented by man! It is much safer in the front line in a war than it is on the roads of this country in peacetime when the automobiles are going full tilt.

I have had several sessions on that subject in Washington, in an endeavor to remedy the situation. I wish the Congress would go into this health situation and pass an intelligent health bill for the benefit of the whole country, so everybody could get medical care at reasonable prices when he needs it.

I appointed a commission to make a survey of the educational situation in this country. That commission made a formidable report and pointed out exactly what the conditions in the schools in this country are today. And I made a recommendation to the Congress that the federal government make a contribution to the support of the schools of the nation.

No action. No action. It's the most disgraceful thing in this country that the teachers of this country are not adequately paid. There are conditions in nearly all public schools in the country where the teacher has so many pupils under her care that she doesn't have time to learn all their names. Something must be done about that!

The bill has passed the Senate. It wouldn't take ten minutes for it to pass the House, if they weren't roosting on it over there. They should stay in session until they pass a bill for the assistance of education in this country.

Now, I have sent a special message to the Congress on agriculture. I made a speech on the agricultural program at Omaha, Nebraska, on a national hookup, on all four networks, and I set out very clearly in that statement, and in the message which I had sent to the Congress, what the agricultural program of this country should be. You know, those support prices for agriculture will expire at the end of this year.

Now, there is a bill pending before the Congress which is adequate to meet the situation, if we could only get it passed. A lot of these gentlemen who are interested in taking over the residence of the president of the United States in 1949 have been out in the farm belt telling the people what is necessary for a farm program and how strongly they are for it. Now, some of these people have powerful influence in this 80th Congress, and if they really mean what they say, they should do something about it. They can do something about it. There is plenty of time.

You see, unless this price support bill is passed, the farm situation can very easily go back to what it was in the 1920s when the farmers had about $4,700 million in income against a $30 billion income last year. Then the farmer didn't have a dime in the bank — if he had money to put in the bank, he would be afraid to go and put it in at that time. He now has $23 billion in the bank — $23 billion in the bank — and he is not afraid of losing it, for there hasn't been a bank failure in this country in three years.

Now, you have got something down here that you are vitally interested in, and I am vitally interested in it, and so is the whole of the West. I have told the people all over the country that the most valuable thing west of the hundredth meridian is water, and that the proper development and control of the water resources of that area are more important to that one-third area of the nation than any other one thing in the country, for without water you can't exist. I always considered this of vital importance to this part of the country, and I have made recommendations on three separate occasions in the budget in regard to that. And this Congress last year cut that budget appropriations, and they cut this one but they didn't cut it quite as much, because — well, this is 1948! It makes a difference!

You know, Daniel Webster, when the United States was trying to build the Pacific Railroad, made the statement in the Senate along in 1830 that the West wasn't any good, and the further it could be kept from the east coast of the United States, the better off the country would be. And there are a lot of Republicans now ready to believe like old Daniel Webster did!

But money spent on reclamation and public power and irrigation is an investment. It gives a return of the money to the Treasury of the United States. It creates more agricultural production, and had it not been for the tremendous agricultural production of this part of the country, and the Mississippi Valley, this country would have been in an awful fix in the last war.

One of the greatest contributions ever made in the history of the world was made by agriculture during those war years, and they are still making that contribution. For had it not been for the immense crops which we have been able to raise in this country, millions of people would have starved to death.

You know, this country has done something never done before in the history of the world. This country has prevented the conquered nations from starving. During the Napoleonic Wars, millions of people starved to death in Bavaria, in Germany, and in Poland. We have made every effort to prevent people from starving to death after this last terrible war. And I want to see the agricultural sections of this country properly improved. I want to see the water resources of these rivers properly used. I want to see the proper development of the Columbia River Basin, the Central Valley of California, and the Colorado River. I want to see them integrated on a power basis, so that they won't have to have a "brown-out" in California in the summertime.

Now, gentlemen, that is a synopsis of eight important measures in which I am vitally interested. There are several more, but the time is too short, and I don't think I ought to try to inflict any more conversation on you about what Congress ought to do. I think I have made it perfectly plain, in these eight-measure instances.

And I do that in a most kindly frame of mind. I know the majority of the congressmen. As individuals they are fine people. I have some of the best friends in the world in the Congress, but when I speak of the 80th Congress and its accomplishments in the last year and a half, I say that that Congress has not done very much for the benefit of the people.

They have passed a rich man's tax law. They have passed a lot of special legislation that helps special classes. And I am against class legislation, and I have tried to show that in numerous vetoes. And I made this trip so that I could lay before you personally my views on this subject. If I am wrong, you will have a chance to attend to me later on, but if I am not wrong, you ought to attend to somebody else.

Thank you very much.

NOTE: In his opening words the president referred to Joseph Short, president of the National Press Club; Goodwin J. Knight, lieutenant governor of California; and Fletcher Bowron, mayor of Los Angeles.

★ ★ ★ ★ ★ ★ ★ ★ ★ ★ ★ ★ ★ ★ ★ ★ ★ ★

JUNE 15

Rear Platform Remarks

Winslow, Arizona (11 A.M.)

It certainly is a pleasure. Thank you, Governor, very much. I have been going around the country telling the people what I think they should be interested in and giving them my viewpoint on things as they exist. The last set speech was made in Los Angeles, California, and now I am on my way home. I am going back to Independence, Missouri, to see the family and then go on to Washington and finish up the necessary work that has to be done there when the Congress adjourns. I am sincerely hoping that some of the things in which I am vitally interested will be accomplished by that time.

I have had a most pleasant ride across this great state this morning. It certainly is a beautiful country. And I saw those wonderful pine forests and had a chance to take a look at the Navajo reservation about which there has been so much talk and about which we have been trying to do so much.

I am exceedingly fond of your two Arizona senators. They are able and distinguished gentlemen, and they work for the interest of the country and for the interest of Arizona. You have an able congressman, also, from Arizona, with whom I am very well acquainted. I think very highly of him also.

I certainly appreciate this wonderful turnout. It does your heart good, when people are so interested in seeing their chief executive that they are willing to gather around from all the surrounding country, in order that they may see what he looks like.

There have been a great many stories told about the president of the United States. That is one of the privileges of this country, to say what you please about anybody you please — that is, if you can back it up!

You know, the greatest epitaph in the country is here in Arizona. It's in Tombstone, Arizona, and this epitaph says, "Here lies Jack Williams. He done his damnedest." I think that is the greatest epitaph a man could have. Whenever a man does the best he can, then that is all he can do; and that is what our president has been trying to do for the last three years for this country.

I sincerely hope that you will familiarize yourselves with the issues, and when the lines are drawn, after these two great conventions meet, I want you to make up your minds as to what you think is best for the country, and then do just that; and if I have been at all convincing, I know you will do the right thing.

★ Gallup, New Mexico (1:30 P.M.)

Thank you, Governor — thank you very much. My goodness — looks as if everybody in New Mexico is here! I have had a most pleasant trip across Arizona, and I am glad to come into New Mexico now and have a look at New Mexico and New Mexico's leading citizens.

You know, the president has been traveling across the country, giving the people a chance to look at him and having a chance on his own account to look at the people. I have seen a lot of people, I have talked to a lot of people, and a lot of people have talked to me. And I think I have made it perfectly plain just what the issues are before the country now. It is special privilege against the interest of the people as a whole. That is the issue that has been plainly set out in the speeches which I have made at Chicago, at Omaha, at Butte, at Seattle, at Spokane, at San Francisco, and at Los Angeles yesterday afternoon.

I can't tell you how I have appreciated the chance to let people know just where I stand and just what I look like. It may be a disappointment to some people, but at least you will know what sort of man you have for president and just what he stands for. The issues are clearly drawn, and then it is up to you to make up your mind whether you want the special-privilege boys to run the country or whether you want the country to be in the hands of people who are working for you interests.

You are going to elect a senator here this fall. I hated to give him up as secretary of agriculture, because he was a good one. I have another good secretary of agriculture, but I always hate to lose a good man. I was sorry to see Senator Hatch retire from the senate, but I know very well, when Anderson takes his place, that the policies and the outlook in the Senate will be carried on in a manner that will be in the interests of New Mexico.

[At this point the president introduced Mrs. Truman, Margaret Truman, former secretary of agriculture Clinton P. Anderson, Secretary of the Interior Julius A. Krug, and Under Secretary of the Interior Oscar L. Chapman. The president then resumed speaking.]

They all seem to be silent — they are tongue-tied for some reason or other — so I guess I will have to do all the talking. I do appreciate the way the people have turned out, and the way the people have given me their attention, and the way they have listened to what I had to say.

I hope you will inform yourselves thoroughly on the facts as they are, and as I have tried to give them to you, and then use your own judgment, because the judgment of the people as a whole is always good. I have found that to be the truth.

Thank you very much.

★ Albuquerque, New Mexico (5:30 P.M.)

Thank you, Governor — thank you very much. It certainly is a pleasure and a privilege for me to be here today. I am more than happy to be in New Mexico. I am more than happy to be back in Albuquerque again. The first time I ever visited New Mexico was in 1909. My grandmother died when she was ninety-one years old, and one of the witnesses to her will lived in Estancia. We took those depositions in Frank Jenning's office. That has been a long time ago. And I have been back here to New Mexico on numerous occasions since then.

I was here once as the president of the National Old Trails and Roads Association, and we set up a monument to the Pioneer Mother here in Albuquerque. Had a great time on that trip, and I met a lot of people in New Mexico. It looks as if they are all here today.

The mayor informs me that this is the biggest crowd that has ever been in Albuquerque. That certainly is a compliment to me, and I appreciate it.

You know, I started out on this trip with the idea in mind of seeing as many people as I could, and talking to as many people as I could, and letting as many people as possible see me, to see just exactly what I look like. There has been a lot of conversation about what I look like, and what I can do, what I know, and what I don't know; and I thought the people were entitled to know what I am thinking and what I have in mind for the welfare of this country.

The issue now is squarely drawn. I drew that issue at Chicago and Omaha and Butte and Spokane and Seattle and Tacoma and Portland and San Francisco and Los Angeles and here. They know now what I stand for and what I have been trying to do. I have been pouring it on them, and they have got the jitters back there. They have gone to work — they have gone to work!

But I haven't been pouring anything on, only what ought to be poured on. The issue in this country is between special privilege and the people. I think I represent the people, and I am trying to tell the people just how I represent them.

For instance, you have an interest in flood control and irrigation and reclamation, and they are all of interest to a number of the great states in this Union. I have been visiting a number of those states that are interested in flood control and irrigation and reclamation, and I have been trying to get action on a project here on the Rio Grande. It has passed the Senate. We hope it will pass the House. That is one of the reasons I came here: I wanted to needle them a little bit, to see if they won't get that project started.

Then you have another interest in this part of the world, and that is the cattle industry. We are short of beef in this country and in all the world, and I hope we can find a way to improve the situation so that we may increase the cattle product of this part of the world.

I know something about cattle in this part of the world, for my old uncle used to have a ranch down here, and he had a lot of cattle, and used to ship it to Kansas City. I remember that one time he shipped a trainload of cattle to Kansas City, and they didn't pay the freight. That was under a Republican administration too. That is not the case now. When you ship a trainload of cattle to Kansas City now, you can buy the train and half the railroad with what you get; and I'm not sorry about that.

NOTE: In the course of his remarks on July 11 the president referred to Arizona governor Dan E. Garvey, New Mexico governor Thomas J. Mabry, and Albuquerque mayor Ernest W. Everly.

★ ★ ★ ★ ★ ★ ★ ★ ★ ★ ★ ★ ★ ★ ★ ★

JUNE 16

Rear Platform Remarks

Dodge City, Kansas (7:30 A.M.)

It looks as if Dodge City really wanted to see what their president looked like. I used to come over here to Dodge City on road matters for the National Old Trails Association. I was the director of that organization, and I have been through here on numerous occasions on work for that organization.

Those were the days when we didn't have the roads we have now, and when it used to take the Santa Fe Railroad a little longer to go from Kansas City than it does now.

I am most happy that you are willing to give me this most cordial welcome this morning. I think you have a right to see your president, and your president has the right to see you. You have a right to know exactly what I have been trying to tell you in the last few weeks, and I think I have succeeded pretty well.

I have seen, I imagine, about two and a half millions of people. I have talked to a great many people, and a great many people have talked to me, and I think I have found out what the country is thinking about.

I think I have definitely fixed the issues which are before the country now. It is merely the fact: are the special-privilege boys going to run the country, or are the people going to run it? It is up to you to decide if you want special privilege to run it. Then you will know what to do. If you don't want the special-privilege boys to run this country, then it is still up to you to decide what you want to do. I merely wanted to lay before you the facts as they are.

It is almost impossible to get definitely the facts before the people, for the simple reason that there are certain people in the newspaper business and certain people in the radio business who have a distorted view of what the people ought to know and ought to think. I know in this part of the world that you think for yourselves. I hope you will just continue to do that, and I won't have anything to worry about.

It has been a very great pleasure to see you all this morning. I hope when the issues are really drawn, and I am not against the field, I can come out here on a political tour and tell you just exactly what the facts are.

★ ★ ★ ★ ★ ★ ★ ★ ★ ★ ★ ★ ★ ★ ★

JUNE 17

Rear Platform Remarks

Jefferson City, Missouri (10:55 A.M.)

Mr. Mayor, and Governor, and all the distinguished Missouri officials:
It certainly is a pleasure to be here this morning and see so many people, so many people that I know. I think probably I could call half of you by name.

I have been down here on many an occasion, both political and otherwise. I made four campaigns for the Senate in this state — two in the primary and two in the general elections. And in those campaigns I was in Jefferson City each time, and I didn't draw a crowd like this. There must be something about this office that makes the people want to see their president. Of course, they know him just as well, if they hadn't seen him. I am glad we get that way, because it is my business on this trip to keep you informed as to what the issues are before the country.

There is just one big issue; it is the special interests against the people. And the president, being elected by all the people, represents the people. You have now a special-interests Congress. You have that special-interests Congress because only one-third of you voted in the election of 1946, and you are getting just what you deserved. I have no sympathy with you. If you do that again, you will also get what you deserve.

Now, you will have a chance, very shortly, to make a decision as to whether you want people in there, in the Congress, to represent you and to look out for your interests or whether you want to continue the special-interests Congress in force.

Now, there are many fine gentlemen in that Congress, but they are not in the majority. They were overwhelmed in 1946. And that is the reason you are getting the sort of legislation you are getting now. If you will analyze that legislative program, you will find that special interests come first, and the people come second.

Now, if the president doesn't get out and inform the people on what the issues are, then he is not doing his duty; and that is why I took this trip, that is why I went out through the West and the Southwest and the central part of the country, in order that the people might understand just what the issues are.

You are interested in agriculture in this part of the world, to some extent — to a great extent, I think — I know. Now, there has been an agricultural program covering the last twelve years, which has been successful. In 1932 the farm income of the United States was $4,700 million — $4,700 million. In 1947 the farm income was a little over $30 billion, six or seven times as much as it was in 1932. The farmers in 1932 were losing their farms, because the mortgages were coming due so fast we couldn't meet them. Not only were they losing their farms, but they didn't have any money in the bank, and if they had money, they were afraid to go to a bank and put it in for fear it would blow up in their faces. We haven't had a single bank failure in the last three years. Nobody has lost any money in a bank failure in the last three years. And the farmers have $23 billion on deposit in those safe banks. Now the issues are clearly drawn. The agricultural situation was brought about by a program in favor of the farmers. That program — the fundamental basis of that program — will expire on the 31st of December. The bill is resting in the Congress that will meet that situation.

Now, since this trip started, Congress has taken action on some most important measures. They have found that the people are interested in some of these things. And I thought I ought to take this trip before the Congress adjourned, to give them a chance to do something for the people. If they do, I will be just as happy as the people will be. But I don't know; I am very doubtful of what will happen.

I think they will have a convention — two conventions in Philadelphia. The first convention will be controlled by the majority of the present Congress, and they are going to tell you what they have done to the people, not for the people. And if the people believe and act on that information, then as I said a while ago, they will get just what they deserve.

I can't tell you how much I have appreciated the privilege of stopping here to see all my friends in Missouri. Back at Warrensburg and Sedalia, I thought everybody in that part of the state was at each one of those stops, but I was mistaken. They are all here. I don't know how they got here so fast. I do appreciate it, and I hope, when I take a political tour, that I can come back and tell you something more about the issues.

NOTE: In his opening words the president referred to James T. Blair, mayor of Jefferson City, and Phil M. Donnelly, governor of Missouri.

★ ★ ★ ★ ★ ★ ★ ★ ★ ★ ★ ★ ★ ★ ★ ★

JUNE 18

Rear Platform Remarks

York, Pennsylvania (9:20 A.M.)

This certainly, certainly makes me happy to see all these smiling faces here this morning. And I was particularly pleased to be able to meet former mayor Shissler of Lancaster, Pennsylvania. He has been in this world ninety-two years and tells me he has shaken hands with every president of the United States since Lincoln, except Andrew Johnson.

In 1856 — that is the year of his birth — James Buchanan was elected president of the United States from Pennsylvania, and Mr. Shissler tells me that he began by shaking hands with James Buchanan. Now, he must have been a pretty young gentleman then. He was twelve years old when he died.

Just think, in 1856, the country at that time was faced with its greatest crisis; in fact, the country at that time was on the verge of one of the most unnecessary wars that we ever fought, the War between the States. And Mr. Shissler was four years old when that war started, and when Lincoln was inaugurated as president of the United States.

Just think what we have gone through since the birth of this grand old man. It is a pleasure and a privilege to me to get a chance to talk to him and to meet him; and I never saw anybody as lively or so well informed on current events as Mr. Shissler is. He has been talking to me about what I ought to do to make this thing work, and his advice is good, because he is speaking from experience. I am delighted, and I can't tell you how highly pleased I am to have this privilege. A man of experience can always tell a younger man what to do and how to do it. If you just listen, sometimes you can get ideas that will work.

I have had a most pleasant trip across the United States and back. In every city, people have turned out, just as you have here, in order to see the president and to hear the president, and understand his viewpoint. That is my errand across the nation. And if it is getting results, I am extremely happy. And I think it is getting results. I should be back in Washington this morning about 12:30, and then I shall have to go to work as usual.

You know, the routine of the president is a steady one. I am an early riser. I usually get up about 5:30 in the morning and go to work about 6 — sitting at my desk in the study, they call it, until 8:00, when I have breakfast. In the meantime, sometimes I take a half hour's walk. These photographers and newspapermen decided one morning that they would take a walk with me. They haven't been back since!

Then I go to the office after breakfast and stay there until 1:00, go back to the office at 3:00 and stay there until the day's work is done, then go back over to the study and stay there until 11:00; then go to bed and get up and do it all over again.

It has certainly been a relief to me, and an education to me, to get out and see the people and to hear what the people have to say. I have addressed immense audiences on this trip, and more people have seen me than have seen any other president in history on any one trip. And I have had a chance to talk to people, and they have had a chance to talk to me, and we understand each other much better. They understand that the president is elected by all the people. He is the only public official who is elected by all the people, and if he doesn't look after the interests of all the people, nobody is going to do it.

I am trying to do just that, for you. And if I have been successful in bringing the issues a little more clearly out into the open, the trip has been worth it just for that.

As I said, I am going back to Washington and go to work and do the level best I can to keep looking after the interests of the people. This is a case of special interests against the people. We have never had a special-interests Congress equal to this one, as the record will show, if you will only study it. That was brought about, of course, because one-third of you stayed at home, and you got just exactly what you deserved, when you got this Congress.

Well now, you are going to have another opportunity. This is 1948! You can tell it is 1948 if you read the *Congressional Record*. And you are going to have the same privilege again, only this time you are going to elect one-third of the Senate, all the House of Representatives, most of your local officials, and you are going to elect the president and vice president of the United States. And if you don't turn out 100 percent and do your duty on election day, you will still be entitled to what you get, because the people of this country are the government, and when they make up their minds what they want, they usually get it.

I just went around over the country to let you know what I think, and what I stand for, and if that is what you believe in, that will be all right. If it isn't, it will be all right too. It will have to be.

But I know that you are most interested in the welfare of this nation. This is the greatest nation in the history of the world. We have attained leadership in the world, attained by no other nation in the history of the world. We must maintain that leadership. We must have the spiritual values that will give us the ability to maintain that leadership, in a manner that will bring peace to the world.

Everybody — everybody without exception — wants peace in the world. That is what we have been striving for ever since the Germans and the Japs folded up. We have been working for peace. We have had some obstructions to attaining that peace, but there is one thing certain: we are unanimously for the foreign policy of the United States. This is one issue which is bipartisan, and that partisanship should stop at the water's edge; and it has stopped just there.

We are trying manfully to maintain that situation in the world which will make the United Nations the means of attaining peace and of settling differences between nations without going to war. That is my one ambition. That is what I have been working for ever since I have been president. I went to San Francisco when the United Nations Charter was finished and witnessed the signing of it. I went to San Francisco and Berkeley, California, right across the bay from San Francisco, just the other day and restated the foreign policy of the United States. And that foreign policy must be maintained by all the people. And I am sure that is exactly what you want to do, because that means peace in the world.

Again, I want to thank you for this cordial welcome and for the privilege of meeting this grand old man and having him give me advice and his experience from Buchanan to the present day. Thank you very much.

★ Baltimore (End of the Tour; 11 A.M.)

Mr. Mayor and my friends in Baltimore:

It certainly is a fine thing to me to receive a welcome like this in Maryland's first city, and particularly from your great mayor, whom I have known for many years in the Congress.

I have had a grand trip, and this is a wonderful windup to that trip. Every city in which I have been has been just as cordial and as enthusiastic as it could be. I have never seen so many smiling faces in my life. I have never had such a welcome from one end of the country to the other as I have had on this tour.

I think it has been constructive. I think it has been necessary for the welfare of the country that I should go and talk to the people and let the people talk to me. I think I have seen more people on this trip than any other president ever saw on any one trip.

I have talked to more people, and more people have talked to me. It has given me a cross section of what people are thinking. It has given me an opportunity to go back to Washington and do a better and more constructive job.

I can't tell you how very much I appreciate this cordial welcome you have

Ending his cross-country tour in Baltimore, Truman said, "I think it has been necessary for the welfare of the country that I should go and talk to the people and let the people talk to me." (Chicago Sun-Times)

given me and how highly pleased I am with it. It is certainly kind of the city of Baltimore and Baltimore's mayor to turn out this way. I thank you from the bottom of my heart.

NOTE: In the course of his remarks on June 18 the president referred to Simon Shissler, former mayor of Lancaster, Pennsylvania, and Thomas D'Alesandro Jr., mayor of Baltimore.

JULY 15

Acceptance Speech, Democratic National Convention

Convention Hall, Philadelphia (2 A.M.)

I am sorry that the microphones are in the way, but I must leave them the way they are because I have got to be able to see what I am doing — as I am always able to see what I am doing.

I can't tell you how very much I appreciate the honor which you have just conferred upon me. I shall continue to try to deserve it.

I accept the nomination.

And I want to thank this convention for its unanimous nomination of my good friend and colleague, Senator Barkley of Kentucky. He is a great man and a great public servant. Senator Barkley and I will win this election and make these Republicans like it — don't you forget that! We will do that because they are wrong and we are right, and I will prove it to you in just a few minutes.

This convention met to express the will and reaffirm the beliefs of the Democratic Party. There have been differences of opinion, and that is the democratic way. Those differences have been settled by a majority vote, as they should be. Now it is time for us to get together and beat the common enemy. And that is up to you.

We have been working together for victory in a great cause. Victory has become a habit of our party. It has been elected four times in succession, and I am convinced it will be elected a fifth time next November.

The reason is that the people know that the Democratic Party is the people's party, and the Republican Party is the party of special interests, and it always has been, always will be.

HST and his running mate, Senator Alben W. Barkley, rallied the party faithful at the 1948 Democratic National Convention. (Truman Library)

The record of the Democratic Party is written in the accomplishments of the last sixteen years. I don't need to repeat them. They have been very ably placed before this convention by the keynote speaker and the candidate for vice president and by the permanent chairman.

Confidence and security have been brought to the people by the Democratic Party. Farm income has increased from less than $2½ billion in 1932 to more than $18 billion in 1947. Never in the world were the farmers of any republic or any kingdom or any other country as prosperous as the farmers of the United States; and if they don't do their duty by the Democratic Party, they are the most ungrateful people in the world!

Wages and salaries in this country have increased from $29 billion in 1933 to more than $128 billion in 1947. That's labor, and labor never had but one friend in politics, and that is the Democratic Party and Franklin D. Roosevelt. And I say to labor what I have said to the farmers: they are the most ungrateful people in the world if they pass the Democratic Party by this year.

The total national income has increased from less than $40 billion in 1933 to $203 billion in 1947, the greatest in all the history of the world. These benefits have been spread to all the people, because it is the business of the Democratic Party to see that the people get a fair share of these things.

The last, worst, 80th Congress proved just the opposite for the Republicans.

The record on foreign policy of the Democratic Party is that the United States has been turned away permanently from isolationism, and we have converted the greatest and best of the Republicans to our viewpoint on that subject.

The United States has to accept its full responsibility for leadership in international affairs. We have been the backers and the people who organized and started the United Nations, first started under the great Democratic president Woodrow Wilson as the League of Nations. The League was sabotaged by Republicans in 1920. And we must see that the United Nations continues as a strong and growing body, so we can have everlasting peace in the world.

We have removed trade barriers in the world, which is the best asset we can have for peace. Those trade barriers must not be put back into operation again.

We have started the foreign aid program, which means the recovery of Europe and China and the Far East. We instituted the program for Greece and Turkey, and I will say to you that all these things were done in a cooperative and bipartisan manner. The Foreign Relations Committees of the Senate and House were taken into the full confidence of the president in every one of these moves, and don't let anybody tell you anything else.

As I have said time and time again, foreign policy should be the policy of the whole nation and not the policy of one party or the other. Partisanship should stop at the water's edge; and I shall continue to preach that through this whole campaign.

I would like to say a word or two now on what I think the Republican philosophy is; and I will speak from actions and from history and from experience.

The situation in 1932 was due to the policies of the Republican Party control of the government of the United States. The Republican Party, as I said a while ago, favors the privileged few and not the common everyday man. Ever since its inception, that party has been under the control of special privilege; and they have completely proved it in the 80th Congress. They proved by the things they did to the people and not for them. They proved it by the things they failed to do. Now, let's look at some of them — just a few.

Time and time again I recommended extension of price control before it expired June 30, 1946. I asked for that extension in September 1945, in November 1945, in a Message on the State of the Union in 1946; and that price control legislation did not come to my desk until June 30, 1946, on the day on which it was supposed to expire. And it was such a rotten bill that I couldn't sign it. And thirty days after that, they sent me one just as bad. I had to sign it, because they quit and went home.

They said, when OPA [Office of Price Administration] died, that prices would adjust themselves for the benefit of the country. They have been adjusting themselves all right! They have gone all the way off the chart in adjusting themselves, at the expense of the consumer and for the benefit of the people that hold the goods.

I called a special session of the Congress in November 1947 — November 17, 1947 — and I set out a ten-point program for the welfare and benefit of this country — among other things, standby controls. I got nothing. Congress has still done nothing.

Way back four and a half years ago, while I was in the Senate, we passed a housing bill in the Senate known as the Wagner-Ellender-Taft bill. It was a bill to clear the slums in the big cities and to help to erect low-rent housing. That bill, as I said, passed the Senate four years ago. It died in the House.

That bill was reintroduced in the 80th Congress as the Taft-Ellender-Wagner bill. The name was slightly changed, but it is practically the same bill. And it passed the Senate, but it was allowed to die in the House of Representatives; and they sat on that bill, and finally forced it out of the Banking and Currency Committee, and the Rules Committee took charge, and it still is in the Rules Committee.

But desperate pleas from Philadelphia in that convention that met here three weeks ago couldn't get that housing bill passed. They passed a bill they called a housing bill, which isn't worth the paper it's written on.

In the field of labor we needed moderate legislation to promote labor-management harmony, but Congress passed instead that so-called Taft-Hartley Act, which has disrupted labor-management relations and will cause strife and bitterness for years to come if it is not repealed, and the Democratic platform says it ought to be repealed.

On the Labor Department, the Republican platform of 1944 said, if they were in power, that they would build up a strong Labor Department. They have simply torn it up. Only one bureau is left that is functioning, and they cut the appropriation of that so it can hardly function.

I recommended an increase in the minimum wage. What did I get? Nothing. Absolutely nothing.

I suggested that the schools in this country are crowded, teachers underpaid, and that there is a shortage of teachers. One of our greatest national needs is more and better schools. I urged the Congress to provide $300 million to aid the states in the present educational crisis. Congress did nothing about it. Time and again I have recommended improvements in the Social Security law, including extending protection to those not now covered, and increasing the amount of benefits, to reduce the eligibility age of women from sixty-five to sixty years. Congress studied the matter for two years but couldn't find the time to extend or increase the benefits. But they did find time to take Social Security benefits away from 750,000 people, and they passed that over my veto.

I have repeatedly asked the Congress to pass a health program. The nation suffers from lack of medical care. That situation can be remedied anytime the Congress wants to act upon it.

Everybody knows that I recommended to the Congress the civil rights program. I did that because I believed it to be my duty under the Constitution. Some of the members of my own party disagree with me violently on this matter. But they stand up and do it openly! People can tell where they stand. But the Republicans all professed to be for these measures. But Congress failed to act. They had enough men to do it; they could have had cloture; they didn't have to have a filibuster. They had enough people in that Congress who would vote for cloture.

Now, everybody likes to have low taxes, but we must reduce the national debt in times of prosperity. And when tax relief can be given, it ought to go to those who need it most, and not those who need it least, as this Republican rich-man's tax bill did when they passed it over my veto on the third try. The first one of these was so rotten that they couldn't even stomach it themselves. They finally did send one that was somewhat improved, but it still helps the rich and sticks a knife into the back of the poor.

Now, the Republicans came here a few weeks ago, and they wrote a platform. I hope you have all read that platform. They adopted the platform, and that platform had a lot of promises and statements of what the Republican Party is for and what they would do if they were in power. They promised to do in that platform a lot of things I have been asking them to do that they have refused to do when they had the power.

The Republican platform cries about cruelly high prices. I have been trying to get them to do something about high prices ever since they met the first time.

Now listen! This is equally as bad and as cynical. The Republican platform comes out for slum clearance and low-rental housing. I have been trying to get them to pass that housing bill ever since they met the first time, and it is still resting in the Rules Committee, that bill.

The Republican platform favors educational opportunity and promotion of education. I have been trying to get Congress to do something about that ever since they came there, and that bill is at rest in the House of Representatives.

The Republican platform is for extending and increasing Social Security benefits. Think of that! Increasing Social Security benefits! Yet when they had the opportunity, they took 750,000 off the Social Security rolls! I wonder if they think they can fool the people of the United States with such poppycock as that!

There is a long list of these promises in that Republican platform. If it weren't so late, I would tell you all about them. I have discussed a number of these failures of the Republican 80th Congress. Every one of them is important. Two of them are of major concern to nearly every American family.

They failed to do anything about high prices; they failed to do anything about housing.

My duty as president requires that I use every means within my power to get the laws the people need on matters of such importance and urgency. I am therefore calling this Congress back into session July 26. On the 26th day of July, which out in Missouri we call Turnip Day, I am going to call Congress back and ask them to pass laws to halt rising prices, to meet the housing crisis — which they are saying they are for in their platform.

At the same time I shall ask them to act upon other vitally needed measures such as aid to education, which they say they are for; a national health program; civil rights legislation, which they say they are for; an increase in the minimum wage, which I doubt very much they are for; extension of the Social Security coverage and increased benefits, which they say they are for; funds for projects needed in our program to provide public power and cheap electricity. By indirection, this 80th Congress has tried to sabotage the power policies the United States has pursued for fourteen years. That power lobby is as bad as the real estate lobby, which is sitting on the housing bill. I shall ask adequate and decent laws for displaced persons in place of this anti-Semitic, anti-Catholic law, which this 80th Congress passed.

Now, my friends, if there is any reality behind that Republican platform, we ought to get some action from a short session of the 80th Congress. They can do this job in fifteen days, if they want to do it. They will still have time to go out and run for office.

They are going to try to dodge their responsibility. They are going to drag all the red herrings they can across the campaign, but I am here to say that Senator Barkley and I are not going to let them get away with it.

Now, what that worst, 80th Congress does in this special session will be the test. The American people will not decide by listening to mere words or by reading a mere platform. They will decide on the record, the record as it has been written. And in the records is the stark truth, that the battle lines of 1948 are the same as they were in 1932, when the nation lay prostrate and helpless as a result of Republican misrule and inaction.

In 1932 we were attacking the citadel of special privilege and greed. We were fighting to drive the money changers from the temple. Today, in 1948, we are now the defenders of the stronghold of democracy and of equal opportunity, the haven of the ordinary people of this land and not of the favored classes or the powerful few. The battle cry is just the same now as it was in 1932, and I paraphrase the words of Franklin D. Roosevelt as he issued the challenge, in accepting nomination in Chicago: "This is more than a political call to arms. Give me your help, not to win votes alone, but to win in this new crusade to keep America secure and safe for its own people."

Now, my friends, with the help of God and the wholehearted push which you can put behind this campaign, we can save this country from a continuation of the 80th Congress and from misrule from now on.

I must have your help. You must get in and push, and win this election. The country can't afford another Republican Congress.

NOTE: This address was carried on a nationwide radio broadcast.

★ ★ ★ ★ ★ ★ ★ ★ ★ ★ ★ ★ ★ ★ ★ ★ ★

SEPTEMBER 6

Labor Day Address

Cadillac Square, Detroit (1:40 P.M.)

Mr. Mayor, distinguished leaders of labor, and fellow citizens:
This, in my opinion, is a great day for labor. This is a great day for the country. When I can stand on this same platform in the city of Detroit with the mayor and with Walter Reuther and Frank Martel, I know the country is on the road to recovery.

I am more than happy to join in this Labor Day celebration. I am more than happy to be present with the CIO and the AF of L in marching together side by side in the interests of the welfare of the country's citizens.

In unity there is strength. Working people need every ounce of strength they possess to meet today's problems. Forces in the world and in our government would destroy free labor. Therefore, I am urging you, with everything I have, to send Frank Hook to the Senate of the United States and to send a congressman from Michigan who will go along with me on the program.

As you know, I speak plainly sometimes. In fact, I speak bluntly sometimes. I am going to speak plainly and bluntly today. These are critical times for labor and for all who work. There is great danger ahead. Right now, the whole future of labor is wrapped up in one simple proposition.

If, in this next election, you get a Congress and an administration friendly

"These are critical times for labor and for all who work," Truman asserted on Labor Day at Detroit's Cadillac Square. "There is great danger ahead." (Chicago Sun-Times)

to labor, you have much to hope for. If you get an administration and a Congress unfriendly to labor, you have much to fear, and you had better look out.

I believe that a strong and free labor movement constitutes a tremendous force for preserving our form of government. A free and strong labor movement. A free and strong labor movement is our best bulwark against communism. To remain strong and free, you must have a friendly administration and a friendly Congress.

There is only one test of friendship. It is a test of the heart. You know without being told who is your friend and who is not your friend. Glance back over the years between 1900 and 1933. Labor was dealt three major blows. In each case these blows coincided with depressions which occurred under Republican administrations and Republican Congresses.

In the depression years of 1907 and 1908, sweeping injunctions were used against labor and sent its trusted leaders to jail. But another blow to the heart of labor came in 1921 when the Republican depression put nearly six million workers out of employment. The strength of labor organizations dropped off, and vicious campaigns of anti-labor propaganda swept the country. It was an era of the open shop and the yellow-dog contract.

A few years passed, and you all remember came the Republican panic of 1930 and the Great Depression, which dealt the workers of the country a terrible blow. There was no unemployment compensation under the Republicans. There was no floor under wages under the Republicans. Average hourly earnings in 1932 were only 45 cents under the Republicans. From twelve to fifteen million workers were out of work and unemployed under the Republicans.

And then in 1933 came the administration of Franklin D. Roosevelt.

For the first time, labor received the recognition and encouragement that it merits. By constructive legislation, President Roosevelt and a sympathetic Congress corrected many of the abuses against which labor had been contending. That Democratic administration, of which I was a party from 1935, passed the Wagner Act to assure fair collective bargaining, abolished the sweatshop, provided unemployment compensation, passed the Social Security Act, saved millions of workers' homes from foreclosure, brought the average wage from 45 cents to $1.33 per hour.

You all remember how a Democratic administration turned the greatest depression in history into the most prosperous era the country has ever seen. Sixty-one million people are employed today. The gains of labor were not accomplished at the expense of the rest of the nation. Labor gains contributed to the nation's general prosperity. Incomes of farmers and businessmen are higher than ever before in the history of the world. But we still have to fight to keep the gains that we have made in the last sixteen years. The plain fact is that these gains are under heavy attack by the spokesmen of reaction.

Two years ago the people of this country, and many workingmen among them, seemed to feel that they wanted a change. They elected the Republican 80th Congress — and they got their change. That Congress promptly fell into the familiar Republican pattern of aid for big business and attack on labor. The Republicans promptly voted themselves a cut in taxes and voted you a cut in freedom.

That 80th Republican Congress failed to crack down on prices, but it cracked down on labor all right! The Republicans failed to give the consumers of America protection against the rising cost of living, but at the same time they put a dangerous weapon into the hands of the big corporations in the shape of the Taft-Hartley law, which I vetoed but which was passed over my veto. The union men with whom I have talked tell me that labor is just beginning to feel the effects of the Taft-Hartley law. And you and I know that the Taft-Hartley law is only a foretaste of what you will get if the Republican reaction is allowed to continue to grow.

Important Republican newspapers have already announced in plain language that Republicans in Congress are preparing further and stronger measures against labor. If the congressional elements that made the Taft-Hartley law are allowed to remain in power, and if these elements are further encouraged by the election of a Republican president, you men of labor can expect to be hit by a steady barrage of body blows. And if you stay at home, as you did in 1946, and keep these reactionaries in power, you will deserve every blow you get.

Not only the labor union but all men and women who work are in danger, and the danger is greatest for those who do not belong to unions. If anything, the blows will fall most severely on the white-collar workers and the unorganized workers.

And that is not all! If this Taft-Hartley law remains in effect, labor's position will be bad enough. But suppose, while that law is in effect, a reactionary Republican administration were to bring upon us another "boom and bust" cycle similar to that which struck us during the last Republican administration?

I don't have to tell you that is an exceedingly real possibility if the Republicans get control of this country again. You can already see signs of it. The "boom" is on for them, and the "bust" has begun for you.

If you let the Republican administration reactionaries get complete control of this government, the position of labor will be so greatly weakened that I would fear, not only for the wages and living standards of the American workingman but even for our Democratic institutions of free labor and free enterprise.

Remember that the reactionary of today is a shrewd man. He is in many ways much shrewder than the reactionaries of the twenties. He is a man with a calculating machine where his heart ought to be. He has learned a great deal about how to get his way by observing demagogues and reactionaries in other countries. And now he has many able allies in the press and in the radio.

If you place the government of this country under the control of those who hate labor, who can you blame if measures are thereafter adopted to destroy the powers, prestige, and earning power of labor?

I tell you that labor must fight now harder than ever before to make sure that its rights are kept intact. In practical terms, this means a powerful political effort which must culminate in an all-out vote on election day. Anything short of an all-out vote would be a betrayal by labor of its own interests.

It is not only the rights of the unions which are at stake but the standard of living of your families. If prices are permitted to rise unchecked, it is your wives and your children who will suffer. As real wages decline in the face of rising prices, it is the housewife who must try desperately to feed and clothe her family while her buying power is steadily whittled away.

My sympathy is with those best of business managers — the wives and mothers of this nation. Think how they have made the pay envelope stretch with each rise in prices. Now Mother has to outfit the children for school at outrageous prices. How she does it, I don't know. I tried to help her out in this terrible price situation, but I got absolutely no help from that "do-nothing" 80th Republican Congress.

Make no mistake, you are face to face with a struggle to preserve the very foundations of your rights and your standards of living. If we were to have a reactionary administration in the years ahead, labor could be only on the defensive, fighting a losing fight. If you produce a smashing victory at the polls, you have much to hope for.

Given such a victory, I foresee the time, and not far off, when it will be possible to develop a new and sounder program of labor relations for the nation, when it will be possible for labor to obtain a more equitable share of the nation's increased productivity than it ever has had. As a basis for such a new program of labor relations, I think it is clear that labor will need to link its position more closely with that of the farmers and the small businessman. I know from my own experience with labor leaders and unions that the ability of labor to discipline itself and to cooperate with other groups in the country is steadily growing.

During the war, when I was surveying American industry as chairman of the Senate Investigation Committee, I came to know the conditions under which labor works and lives. I came to know and respect the minds and spirit of workers and union leaders. I saw them and talked to them and visited their homes in scores of communities. I watched them at work in hundreds of plants. I know that labor is just as willing as any other group in the country to cooperate with intelligent programs in the interest of the nation as a whole.

I am one of those who believes in the fundamental good sense and good feeling of the American people. It is my conviction that Republican reaction will be rejected. The American public wants a Congress and an administration that will play fair with labor. The people will support a program under which labor makes gains consistent with the progress of our total economy.

I said a moment ago that the public is full of good feeling and good sense. That is certainly true of the great majority. Nevertheless, I must point out that there are too many shortsighted and unthinking Americans who have adopted a "damn labor" attitude, which doesn't become any citizen of this country.

It is time that every American recognize what our fathers knew — that it is an honorable thing to work with your hands. Our basic social freedoms can be traced largely to the fact that labor had its birth of real freedom in the United States of America. That is why our fathers came to America — to find the country where the man who worked with his hands is as good as the next man.

Today too many Americans in dining cars, in country clubs, and fashionable resorts are repeating, like parrots, the phrase "Labor must be kept in its place." It is time that all Americans realized that the place of labor is side by side with the businessman and with the farmer, and not one degree lower.

One of the aspects of this Taft-Hartley agitation that has been most shocking to me has been the Republican attitude as expressed in the pious speeches of some of their leaders in government and in business. They seem to think that labor is some kind of a spoiled child that needs to be spanked. They lift their eyes sympathetically and say, "It hurts me more than it hurts you." It does hurt you.

In practical terms, it means that labor needs to unite in common causes. They must unite, and it will be a great day for labor and a great day for the country when that happens.

All of labor stands at the crossroads today. You can elect a reactionary administration. You can elect a Congress and an administration which stand ready to play fair with every element in American life and enter a new period of hope. The choice is yours.

Do you want to carry the Taft-Hartley law to its full implication and enslave totally the workingman, white-collar and union man alike, or do you want to go forward with an administration whose interest is the welfare of the common man?

Labor has always had to fight for its gains. Now you are fighting for the whole future of the labor movement. We are in a hard, tough fight against shrewd and rich opponents. They know they can't count on your vote. Their only hope is that you won't vote at all. They have misjudged you. I know that we are going to win this crusade for the right!

NOTE: In his opening words the president referred to Eugene I. Van Antwerp, mayor of Detroit; Walter Reuther, president of the United Automobile Workers; and Frank Martel, president of the Detroit and Wayne County Federation of Labor. The address was carried on a nationwide radio broadcast.

SEPTEMBER 18

Rear Platform Remarks
Rock Island, Illinois (5:45 A.M.)

I don't think I have ever seen so many farmers in town in all my life. I had no idea that there would be anybody else in a town the size of Rock Island at this time of day.

It is a pleasure for me to be here with you, and I am highly honored to be introduced by the next senator from Illinois, and I am highly honored to

Truman sensed that the tide was beginning to turn when a huge crowd showed up for a 5:45 A.M. whistle-stop appearance in Rock Island, Illinois. Others on the rear platform include, left to right: downstate Democratic leader Bernard Moran; Ora Smith, nominee for Illinois state treasurer; and (behind the microphone), Paul H. Douglas, nominee from Illinois for the U.S. Senate. (Chicago Sun-Times)

have alongside me the next senator from Iowa, Guy Gillette. Senator Gillette and I served in the Senate, and Douglas — I never had the pleasure of serving with Senator-to-be Douglas, but I will probably have a chance to associate with him a very great deal the next four years.

You know the issues in this campaign are not hard to define. The issue is the people against the special interests, and if you need any proof of that, all you need to do is to review the record of this Republican 80th Congress.

You remember in 1946, when everybody said he wanted a change, that he thought the country had had enough, and they put out such propaganda as that, most of you stayed at home, and by a minority vote of about a third of the voters, you elected a Congress that I think has given you enough!

The object of this 80th Congress, it seemed to me, was to take the bargaining power away from labor and give it back to the special interests. It was also the idea of the lobbies that controlled that 80th Congress to see that prices were not controlled. You know, I think they really like to have a "boom and bust." You know, that Congress had some of the most terrific lobbies that have ever been in Washington in the history of the country. They had the real estate lobby, the one that turned the rent control program loose, and they had the speculators lobby, and they had the National Association of Manufacturers lobby, whose interest is not the public interest — it is special interest.

I want to bring it home to you that you must yourselves analyze the condition of the country over a sixteen-year period, fourteen years of which were in the hands of a Democratic administration. You must also go back and compare that situation with the one with which we were faced after twelve years of "normalcy." Shall we call it?

That is what they want to go back to. We don't want to go back, we want to go forward!

Dozens of times — I won't say that; at least half a dozen times, I'll say — I asked the Congress to give us a price control bill that would gradually release those controls as production caught up with consumption and prevent a runaway inflation. You were informed by the National Association of Manufacturers in 1946 that within one year prices would adjust themselves. They have adjusted themselves. They have gone all the way off the chart. It has not been in the interests of the common man either. It has been in the interest of special interests who want to control this country again.

Now, you can't afford to let that happen. You must — if you want this country to go forward, you must always be sure that you have people in control of the government whose interest is yours and not the special interests who want special privilege in everything that takes place.

Now, in order to prevent that, you must elect men like Senator Douglas here in Illinois and men like Senator Gillette in Iowa. You must elect congressmen whose interest is the people's interest and not special-privilege interests. I hope you will do that on November 2.

In order to get that done, you have got to get on the books and get registered. And you have got to go out and vote on election day. As I told you a while ago, just one-third of the people voted — a light vote — in 1946, and you see what you got. You got the Republican 80th "do-nothing" Congress.

Now, if you are going to stay at home again — if you are going to shirk your public duty again, that is what you will get again, and that is just exactly what you will deserve.

Thank you very much.

SEPTEMBER 18

Address at the National Plowing Match

Dexter, Iowa (12:30 P.M.)

Mr. President, and all the good farmers who are responsible for this wonderful demonstration:

It does my heart good to see the grain fields of the nation again. They are a wonderful sight. The record-breaking harvests you have been getting in recent years have been a blessing. Millions of people have been saved from starvation by the food you have produced. The whole world has reason to be everlastingly grateful to the farmers of the United States.

In a very real sense, the abundant harvests of this country are helping to save the world from communism. Communism thrives on human misery. And the crops you are producing are driving back the tide of misery in many lands. Your farms are a vital element in America's foreign policy. Keep that in mind; that is of vital importance to us and to the world.

And while I am on that subject — I know that the war talk which is so prevalent today is causing all of you deep concern. It is plain enough that we are facing a very disturbing international situation. I should like every American to realize that this country is making every possible effort to preserve the peace.

In this critical situation, my motto has been: "Keep your temper and stand firm." We have kept our tempers. We have stood firm. And we have been reasonable and straightforward at all times.

It is the policy of this government to continue working for peace with every instrument at our command. At the same time, we have been rapidly building up our strength. The peace of the world and the prestige of the United States require that the nation be strong and vigilant.

But that is not the main point I wish to cover today. In addition to the issue of peace, there is another important reason why this is a critical period for America. I am talking about our economic future — your economic future.

Will this nation succeed in keeping its prosperity? Will it preserve its high standards of living next year, and the year after, and the year after that?

I know of only one way to get assured prosperity. That is by cooperation of agriculture with labor, cooperation of agriculture and labor with business, large and small.

When these groups work together in a common cause, this country can achieve miracles. We saw that during the war. We saw it before the war. By common effort, in the last fifteen years, every group in the nation steadily increased its income. Our people rose from despair to the highest living standards in the history of the world.

So long as the farmer, the worker, and the businessman pull together in the national interest, this country has everything to hope for. But it is terribly dangerous to let any one group get too much power in the government. We cannot afford to let one group share the nation's policies in its own interest, at the expense of others.

That is what happened in the 1920s, under the big-business rule of the Republicans. Those were the days when big corporations had things their own way. The policies that Wall Street big business wanted were the policies that the Republicans adopted. Agriculture, labor, and small business played second fiddle, while big business called the tune. Those were the days of Republican high tariffs — tariffs which penalized the American farmer by making him pay high prices for manufactured goods, while he was receiving low prices for his crops.

You remember the results of the Wall Street Republican policy. You remember the big boom and the great crash of 1929. You remember that in 1932 the position of the farmer had become so desperate that there was actual violence in many farming communities. You remember that insurance companies and banks took over much of the land of small independent farmers — 223,000 farmers lost their farms. That was a painful lesson. It should not be forgotten for a moment.

Since then the farmer has come a long way. The agricultural program of the Democratic administration in sixteen years has enabled farmers to attain decent standards of living. Interest rates on farm credit have been sharply brought down. Farm mortgage indebtedness has been reduced by more than 50 percent. Farm mortgage foreclosures have almost disappeared. In 1947 the smallest number of farm foreclosures in the history of the country took place. All this was done under a Democratic administration.

Today the world needs more food than ever before. There is every reason for the American farmer to expect a long period of good prices — if he continues to get a fair deal. His great danger is that he may be voted out of a fair deal and into a Republican deal.

The Wall Street reactionaries are not satisfied with being rich. They want to increase their power and their privileges, regardless of what happens to the other fellow. They are gluttons of privilege.

These gluttons of privilege are now putting up fabulous sums of money to elect a Republican administration. Why do you think they are doing that? For the love of the Republican candidate? Or do you think it is because they expect a Republican administration to carry out their will, as it did in the days of Harding, Coolidge, and Hoover?

I think we know the answer. I think we know that Wall Street expects its money this year to elect a Republican administration that will listen to the gluttons of privilege first and to the people not at all. Republican reactionaries want an administration that will assure privilege for big business, regardless of what may happen to the rest of the nation.

The Republican strategy is to divide the farmer and the industrial worker — to get them to squabbling with each other — so that big business can grasp the balance of power and take the country over, lock, stock, and barrel.

To gain this end, they will stop at nothing. On the one hand, the Republicans are telling industrial workers that the high cost of food in the cities is due to this government's farm policy. On the other hand, the Republicans are telling the farmers that the high cost of manufactured goods on the farm is due to this government's labor policy.

That's plain hokum. It's an old political trick: "If you can't convince 'em, confuse 'em." But this time it won't work.

The farmer and the worker know that their troubles have been coming from another source. Right here I would like to cite you an example of the situation that they were faced with not so long ago. In 1932, under the Republicans, we had 12,500,000 unemployed, with average hourly wages at 45 cents, and we had 15-cent corn and 3-cent hogs. In fact, you burnt up some of your corn because you couldn't market it — it was too cheap.

Those gluttons of privilege remember one plain fact. Never once during the great crises of the past fifty years have the Wall Street Republican administrations lifted a finger to help the farmer. Wait a minute — wait a minute! — they did once. They gave you a Farm Board. That was their great contribution.

How well you must remember the depression of the 1930s! The Republicans gave you that greatest of all depressions, as I said before, when hogs went down to 3 cents, and corn was so cheap you were burning it up.

All through this country, the American farmer and worker have been the victims of boom-and-bust cycles — with accent on the bust, especially for the farmers and the workers. And they have suffered alike in these misfortunes.

I wonder how many times you have to be hit on the head before you find out who's hitting you? It's about time that the people of America realized what the Republicans have been doing to them.

Why is it that the farmer and the worker and the small businessman suffer under Republican administrations and gain under Democratic administrations? I'll tell you why. It is the result of a basic difference in the attitude between the Democratic and the Republican parties.

The Democratic Party represents the people. It is pledged to work for agriculture. It is pledged to work for the small businessman and the white-collar worker. The Democratic Party puts human rights and human welfare first.

But the attitude of the Republican gluttons of privilege is very different. The big-money Republican looks on agriculture and labor merely as expense items in a business venture. He tries to push their share of the national income down as low as possible and increase his own profits. And he looks upon the government as a tool to accomplish this purpose.

These Republican gluttons of privilege are cold men. They are cunning men. And it is their constant aim to put the government of the United States under the control of men like themselves. They want a return of the Wall Street economic dictatorship.

You have had a sample of what the Republican administration would mean to you. Two years ago, in the congressional elections, many Americans decided that they would not bother to vote. Well, others thought they would like to have a change. And they brought into power a Republican Congress — that notorious "do-nothing" 80th Republican Congress.

Let us look at the results of that change. This Republican Congress has already stuck a pitchfork in the farmer's back. They have already done their best to keep the price supports from working. Many growers have sold wheat this summer at less than the support price, because they could not find proper storage.

When the Democratic administration had to face this problem in the past, the government set up grain bins all over the wheat and corn belts to provide storage. Now the farmers need such bins again. But when the Republican Congress rewrote the charter of the Commodity Credit Corporation this year, there were certain lobbyists in Washington representing the speculative grain trade — your old friend.

These big-business lobbyists and speculators persuaded the Congress not to provide the storage bins for the farmers. They tied the hands of the administration. They are preventing us from setting up storage bins that you will need in order to get the support price for your grain. When the farmers have to sell their wheat below the support price, because they have no place to store it, they can thank this same Republican 80th Congress that gave the speculative grain trade a rake-off at your expense.

The Republican reactionaries are not satisfied with that. Now they are attacking the whole structure of price supports for farm products. This attack comes at a time when many farm prices are dropping and the price support program is of the greatest importance to the farmer.

The Democratic Party originated the farm support program. We built the price support plan out of hard experience. We built it for the benefit for the entire nation — not only for the farmer but for the consumer as well.

Republican spokesmen are now complaining that my administration is trying to keep farm prices up. They have given themselves away. They have given you a plain hint of what they have in store for you if they come into power. They are obviously ready to let the bottom drop out of farm prices.

The purpose of price support is to prevent farm prices from falling to ruinously low levels. Every consumer should realize that these supports apply only when farm prices have dropped below parity. The government is not now supporting the price on major food items such as meats, dairy products, and poultry. The government has just begun to support the price of wheat, which has dropped from around $3 a bushel to about $2 a bushel.

This support price has nothing to do with the price the consumer is paying for bread. Now listen to this! When wheat prices were going up, the price of bread rose steadily. It went up from 10 cents a loaf to 13 cents to 14 cents. Now, wheat prices have fallen a dollar a bushel. But the price of bread has come down not one cent!

There you have the policy of the reactionary big business. Pay as little as you can to the farmer, and charge the consumer all he can bear. That is a fair sample of what the Republican reaction has meant to you in the past two years — to you and to every consumer in the cities and on the farms.

When the Republicans claim that the wheat price supports are to blame for the high price of bread, they are trying to stir up the city consumer against the farmer by downright dishonesty. The truth of the matter is that by encouraging the record production of the last few years, the support program has actually kept the consumer prices down. Those who are willfully trying to discredit the price support system don't want the farmers to be prosperous. They believe in low prices for farmers, cheap wage for labor, and high profits for big corporations.

These are the facts the people need to know. I am going to keep hammering away at the facts until the whole country rings with the truth about these gluttons of privilege. The record of the Republican 80th Congress is one long attack on the welfare of the farmer.

Under the Democratic administrations since 1933, the government sponsored the great soil conservation program which helped to lay the foundations for the present prosperity of the American farmer. But that "do-nothing" Republican 80th Congress, under the false mask of economy, cut and threatened to kill the soil conservation program. You people here know best the importance of soil conservation to American agriculture. You bet you do! You know what the reactionary attack on soil conservation will cost the farmer if we let the Republicans have their own way.

At every point the Republican 80th Congress did what the speculative grain lobby wanted it to do. They have killed the International Wheat Agreement, which would have assured the American wheat growers a large export market for five years at fair prices. They started a move to put a death tax on farm cooperatives. They ruled out the grain bins that help make the ever-normal granary effective. They have invited a depression by refusing to curb inflation. And now they are attacking the farm support program.

The Wall Street Republicans are not worrying about whether you like it or not. Their political wiseacres have assured them that the farmer has fallen back into his old habit of voting Republican, whatever happens. The Republicans are saying, "Don't worry about the farm vote. It's in the bag." So long as you had a good year once in a while, you would be satisfied. So they thought. And so they think today.

You and I know they're making a big mistake. From what I have seen, the farmers of this country have their eyes open. You're not going to be fooled again by the slick propaganda of Wall Street.

In only two years, with only the Congress under their control, the Republicans were able to weaken your position gravely. Well, imagine what would happen if they were to get both the Congress and the presidency for four years. What they have taken away from you thus far would be only an appetizer for the economic tapeworm of big business.

Your best protection is to elect a Democratic Congress and a president who will play fair with the farmer — an administration that will reinforce soil conservation, provide adequate storage facilities for grain, encourage production, and help the farmer make enough on his crop to meet the cost of living and have something left over.

I don't need to tell you how long it takes to get a good crop and how big the dangers are. You can work a year, plowing and cultivating, and then at the last minute a sudden drought or flood can wipe you out. You all know how terrible these disasters of nature can be.

Now you are faced with the danger of another kind of disaster — a manmade disaster bearing the Republican trademark. For sixteen years the Democrats have been working on a crop of prosperity for the farmer. We have been plowing and seeding and cultivating the soil of the American economy in order to get a crop of prosperity that you have been enjoying for the past several years. The question is, are you going to let another Republican light wipe out that prosperity?

I have reminded you of the evils wrought by the Republican administrations in recent times. But my purpose has not been merely to bring up the past. I am trying to point the way to a healthy future. The Democratic Party is looking forward, not back. We are planning to aid the farmers of America to meet their pressing problems and avoid catastrophe.

Today farmers are faced with the threat that markets will fail to keep up with their production. The reactionary Republican answer is to let prices crash to the bottom. But the Democratic Party has a constructive way of preventing such a collapse.

We are reaching out to develop world markets that will absorb production above America's own needs. Scientific research is discovering more and newer uses for farm products. We know that the world can absorb the farmers' output, if the right conditions are created, and we are working to ensure continued prosperity for American agriculture.

The Democratic Party is fighting the farmer's battle. We believe that farmers are entitled to share equally with other people in our national income. We believe that a prosperous and productive agriculture is essential to our national welfare.

But the Democratic Party does not stand in defense of the farmer alone. It stands for the people of the United States — the farmer, the industrial worker, and the white-collar worker. Our intentions are made clear by our deeds. In this twentieth century, every great step forward has come during Democratic administrations of the national government. Every movement backward has come under Republican auspices, and it is the people who have paid dearly for these reactionary moves.

Too much is now at stake — here and throughout the world — to take the wrong path now. There is one way to stop the forces of reaction. Get every vote out on election day, and make it count. You can't afford to waste your votes this year.

I'm not asking you just to vote for me. Vote for yourselves! Vote for your farms! Vote for the standard of living that you have won under a Democratic administration! Get out there on election day, and vote for your future!

★ Informal Remarks after the Match (2:15 P.M.)

Thank you very much. I have had a most pleasant day, and outside the fact that I have had to make speeches it has been a happy day.

I heard a fellow tell a story about how he felt when he had to make speeches. It's an old, old story. I heard it about forty years ago. He said when he had to make a speech, he felt like the fellow who was at the funeral of his wife, and the undertaker had asked him if he would ride down to the cemetery in the same car with his mother-in-law. He said, "Well, I can do it, but it's just going to spoil the whole day for me."

I am in sort of that frame of mind, but I have had to make a speech, especially one as important as that one this morning which I made, which outlined the Democratic platform on the farm.

I had a most interesting and educational tour around this plowing contest ground today. I met the owners and tenants of these farms and inquired of them if they thought all of this tramping would ruin this good Iowa soil; and they said, "No, one rain would cure it all." That is remarkable. That is entirely remarkable.

I saw this straight-line plowing contest as we came in and was particularly interested in watching to see whether there were jumps and curves in the furrows. I didn't see any places where it could be said there was a crook in the furrow. They were all so straight. I don't see how they could ever check them.

I went over and looked at the contour plowing, and the uses that were being made of the water holes to stop the wash — most interesting. I was down in the Virgin Islands not long ago, and they are starting that contour treatment of the hills and volcanoes down in that part of the world, and they are raising some remarkable crops on those terraces. So you see, we are using our knowledge not only to improve Iowa and Missouri and Illinois; we are using it to improve those peoples who are dependent upon us for a living and for information on how to make a living.

Your friend who introduced me said that he would like to hear some of my experiences as a farmer. It is hardly worth telling at this age.

[At this point Herbert Plambeck, director of the National Plowing Match, asked the president to comment on a statement that Mr. Truman could "plow one of the straightest furrows of anyone in your community."]

I will tell you frankly, that statement was made by a very, very prejudiced witness. That statement was made by my mother.

I did have a reputation, though, of being able to sow a 160-acre wheat field without a skipped place showing in it. My father used to always raise so much fuss about a skip place in an oat field or a wheat field that I was very careful never to have a skip place. I accomplished it by putting a marker on the drill — it was like planting corn.

I have had some other experiences that are interesting. In those days, we had what we called a gangplow, two 12-inch plows on the same frame with three wheels on it, and the locomotive power was four horses, or four mules, or three mules and a horse, or whatever you could get to pull it. It moved at a rate where it turned over a two-foot furrow, and you could count the revolutions of the big wheel, from which you could tell how long it would take to plow an acre or to plow a field — three or four days, sometimes longer.

Now you can get on a tractor and plow night and day. You don't have to feed it or water it; you can get off it whenever you please, take a nap, come back, and run it again. I didn't live on the farm in this age. I'm sorry I didn't. I don't want to turn the clock back. I don't want to go back to the horse-and-buggy age, although some of our Republican friends do.

[At this point Mr. Plambeck reminded the president that many of the estimated one hundred thousand persons present had arrived since his appearance earlier in the day and were seeing him for the first time. He suggested the president might want to tell them how he felt about "coming back to the land of golden corn and green fields." The president then resumed speaking.]

I will come back anytime you ask me, especially if I am met by ten acres of people. Now, you figure out how many that is!

NOTE: In his main address at the National Plowing Match the president spoke before an audience of over eighty thousand persons. His opening words "Mr. President" referred to Herb Plambeck, director of the match. The main address was carried on a nationwide radio broadcast.

Address at the Colorado State Capitol
Capitol Grounds, Denver (Noon)

Governor, Senator, distinguished politicians, and members of the Democratic Party of Colorado, ladies and gentlemen:

Every time I come out this way I feel again the tremendous vitality of the West. That feeling comes not only from magnificent scenery and bracing air. It comes from talking to the vigorous, confident people who live out here.

This is a straight-from-the-shoulder country, and it has produced a great breed of fighting men. I am going to call upon your fighting qualities now. For you and I have a fight on our hands — a fight for the future of this country and for the welfare of the people of the United States.

The other day, a cartoonist for a Republican newspaper drew a cartoon of me that I enjoyed. He showed me dressed up as Paul Revere, riding through a colonial town yelling to the townspeople: "Look out! The Republicans are coming!"

It was a good cartoon. There's a lot of truth in it. But it's not quite accurate. What I am really telling you is not that the Republicans are coming, but they are here. They have been in Washington for the last two years in the form of the notorious Republican "do-nothing" 80th Congress. Today I want to talk to you about what that Republican Congress has been doing to you and to your families and to your country.

Understand me: when I speak of what the Republicans have been doing, I'm not talking about the average Republican voter. Nobody knows better than I that man for man, individually, most Republicans are fine people. But there's a big distinction between the individual Republican voter and the policies of the Republican Party.

Something happens to Republican leaders when they get control of the government or even of a part of the government — something that shocks and dismays many of their own loyal supporters. Republicans in Washington have a habit of becoming curiously deaf to the voice of the people. They have a hard time hearing what the ordinary people of the country are saying. But they have no trouble at all hearing what Wall Street is saying. They are able to catch the slightest whisper from big business and the special interests.

When I talk to you here today about Republicans, I am talking about the party that gets most of its campaign funds from the special interests in Wall Street. I am talking to you about the party that gave us the phony boom of the 1920s and the Hoover depression which followed it. I am talking to you about the party that gave us that Republican 80th Congress.

The Republican Party today is controlled by silent and cunning men who have a dangerous lust for power and privilege. The Republican Party is fundamentally the party of privilege. These men are now reaching out for the control of the country and its resources.

It is your votes which will decide whether or not they have their way. That is why I have come out here today. I want you to know the facts.

I repeat: the most reactionary elements in the country today are backing the Republican Party in its effort to take over your government on election day. If they succeed, I predict that they will turn back the clock to the day when the West was an economic colony of Wall Street. That is terrible even to contemplate.

Election day this year, your choice will not be merely between political parties. You will be choosing a way of life for years to come. This is a fateful election. On it will depend your standard of living and the economic independence of your community. You can choose to be governed by Republican puppets of big business — the same breed that gave you the worst depression in our history. Or you can choose to be governed by the servants of the people, who are pledged to work for the welfare of all the people, the nominees of the Democratic Party.

Some of you may feel that I am attacking the leaders of the Republican Party rather sharply. I am. And I have good reasons for doing it — reasons like the obstacles placed in the way of conservation of our natural resources; reasons like the housing conditions in this country; reasons like the high cost of living; reasons close to your hearts and to mine.

You people out here have been thinking about these problems. You have a right to know what your government is going to do about them. Let's go into them a little bit. Let's see where the Republicans stand on these vital issues and where the Democratic Party stands.

We all know that the housing situation in this country is a national disgrace. It is almost unbelievable that we should have made so little progress in providing decent housing conditions for millions of American families.

From the first day of that Republican 80th Congress, there was a housing bill before it which would meet the problem. That bill was a full-scale program to provide housing for all our people and not just for those who can pay high prices. But the Republicans refused to act.

The situation became more and more desperate. Veterans' groups, labor groups, mayors of cities, governors of states, pleaded with the Republicans to pass the housing bill. Even that hypocritical Philadelphia convention made a plea for it. Can you beat that? They still did nothing.

The Republican stand on housing was clearly exposed last July, when I called the Congress into special session and demanded again that they enact housing legislation. The bill was ready. It had been studied and discussed times without number. It was supposed to be nonpartisan.

But what happened? There was a certain real estate lobby which had its high-priced agents operating in Washington. These men, representing big real estate interests, were in close touch with the Republican leaders. The Republican leadership in the House of Representatives cracked the whip. And the Republican Senate killed the nonpartisan housing bill.

This was no accident. It was Republican policy. In 1947, Senator Taft joined with two Democratic senators — Senator Wagner and Senator Ellender — in introducing the housing bill. But in 1948 he voted against the bill with his own name on it. What a whip they must have cracked over Taft!

Why did the Republicans kill the bill? The answer is plain. They wanted to leave housing under the control of the profiteers. There is a lot of money to be made out of providing houses for the people — if private interests are allowed to exact exorbitant profits from the people.

Have you felt the pinch of the housing shortage? Put the blame where it belongs. And remember, if the Republicans were to come into power for the next four years, the future of American housing would be in the hands of the same men who killed that housing bill — the men who obey the lobbyists of selfish interest, the powerful real estate lobby, and half a dozen others which I am going to talk to you about later on in this campaign.

Now, about high prices. I know you are troubled by high prices. Well, put the blame where it belongs — on the leaders of the Republican Party. The Republican record in dealing with inflation is typical.

When I called the Republican Congress into special session this year and asked them for price control measures, they said that my request was made for political purposes. They used that as an excuse and did nothing about prices. They very conveniently forgot that I had called a special session of the same Congress in 1947 and asked for the same price control. And 1947 was not an election year.

If they had put into effect the controls I asked for, the prices on such things as meat, milk, steel, and automobiles would have been stabilized or reduced. The Republicans could easily have taken this issue out of politics merely by doing something about it. But they chose to do nothing about it.

I have been talking about the conservation of our economic well-being. Now I come to a particular phase of that conservation that has special interest for you of the West. You live in a region whose whole future depends on its wise use of the rich resources that Nature has provided.

Early in this century, a unique Republican president, Theodore Roosevelt, fought for conservation, only to be repudiated by his party. All through the Republican administrations from 1921 to 1933, the big-business pressure groups prevented adequate conservation measures from being put into effect. They wanted quick profits, the easy way. And so western forests were logged off and left barren. Rangelands were grazed off and ruined. Farmland was worked to the point where its fertility was gone. Precious water ran unused past barren land. There was no soil conservation program, no range conservation program. The nation lost tremendous quantities of its most valuable resources. The West continued to bow to Wall Street — furnishing raw materials at low prices and buying back finished goods at high prices.

Then, in 1933, came the Democratic administration of Franklin D. Roosevelt. Under his leadership, conservation was made a living reality. You know better than anyone how much it has meant to the West.

The Democratic administration won its fight for conservation and for western development against the bitter opposition of Wall Street and the special interests. You of the West see the results of our victory every day. You see those results in bigger and better crops; in new industries; in the growing national parks and forests and the tourists who visit them; in the rising standards of living of the people of the West; and in the stronger economy of the whole nation.

But we still have a long way to go. We are still using our timber faster than we grow it. Thousands of acres of land are still being washed away every year. Disastrous floods are still frequent. Conservation in the West is of first importance to the whole country.

In the face of all this, what did the "do-nothing" Republican Congress do? Remember, the record of that Congress is the actual test of the attitude of the Republican leadership toward the people. The Republicans in Congress consistently tried to cut the ground from under the conservation program. Last year, the Republican-dominated House of Representatives voted to cut the agricultural conservation program in half in 1947 and to end it entirely by 1948.

The Democrats in the Senate led, and finally won, a fight to save the life of that program. They saved it, but they could not completely restore it. The program was seriously damaged by the Republican 80th Congress.

Here is a significant fact. Nineteen forty-seven was the first year in a decade and a half that the Republicans had control of Congress. And that was the first year in which the Congress took a step backward in the field of soil conservation since that program was begun. The first time the Republicans had a chance, they began to undermine conservation.

Now, let's look at another subject that is closely bound up with your future — the industrial development of the West. I know that all of you recognized the importance of creating new industries in this region, using the resources of the West, so as to reduce your industrial dependence upon the East. For my part, I am convinced that rapid and sound industrial development in the West will make a vital contribution to the living standards and the well-being, not only of the people of the West, but of the whole nation.

The heart of the western industrial development program is hydroelectric power. Coupled with the irrigation projects and flood control, electric power is of fundamental importance to your future. The Democratic Party, for the past fifteen years, has been energetically developing the great dams, irrigation projects, and power systems which have contributed so much to the prosperity of the West. But as soon as the Republican Party gained control of the Congress, it began to tear down the whole western development program. The Republicans slashed funds right and left. They cut back projects to bring water to the land and electric power to industry.

Right here in this state, the Colorado–Big Thompson Project is under way. It is an inspiring project, involving the transfer of water from one side of the Continental Divide to the other. The Republican Congress sharply reduced the funds for that project. When I pointed out the danger of that action and requested them to restore those funds, they refused to do it.

Wherever you turn, no matter what field of activity, you find the same story. In the light of the evidence, I say flatly that the Republican leaders have been working against the interests of the people. I say that they have been eager agents of the big-business lobbies and the most reactionary elements in American economic life. They jump for these lobbyists, buy they won't do anything for the people.

In the last sixteen years, Democratic administrations have built a firm foundation for a new and greater West. We restored grazing lands for the sustained production of livestock. Millions of cattle and sheep feed today where only prairie dogs and rattlesnakes existed before. We restored forests for a sustained yield of timber. Trees stand for the future where exploiters would have wiped them out. We established a sound conservation policy to prevent land erosion and restore the fertility of the soil. We built the federal system of hydroelectric and irrigation projects which are now providing water for more than five million irrigated acres in the West and for better living for millions of people. We have been leading the fight for decent housing, effective reduction of the cost of living, and a rise in living standards — all for a better nation of happier people. That is the Democratic record — a record of which I am exceedingly proud.

There is more to do, much more. What we have done so far is only the beginning. This is no time to permit progress to be checked, when you can foresee great new developments of your agriculture, your industry, and your commerce, if you have the aid and support of the federal government. Your need is to ensure the election of an administration pledged to give you that aid and support — in other words, you need a Democratic administration.

There is a hard fight ahead. We shall have to fight the slick political propaganda of the special interests and the Republican leadership. We shall have to fight the millions of dollars that Wall Street is pouring into the treasury of the Republican Party. We shall have to fight the Republican undercover sabotage of the West.

But we of the Democratic Party are eager for that fight. In fact, I am taking it to them right now. We believe that we owe to future generations the bequest of a strong America, mighty in its resources and wise in its use of them. We are firmly determined to leave after us a land that is better than we found it.

NOTE: In his opening words the president referred to Governor William Lee Knous and Senator Edwin C. Johnson, both of Colorado. The address was carried on a nationwide radio broadcast.

SEPTEMBER 21

Address at the Mormon Tabernacle
Salt Lake City (8:03 P.M.)

Governor Maw, President Smith, distinguished guests, citizens of Utah:

It is a pleasure to me to be here this evening. You don't know what a great pleasure it is to see this magnificent auditorium, one of the historic ones in the world, and all these thousands and thousands of people who have taken the trouble to come out to listen to me and to weigh what I have to say. My train trip coming out here across the country has been a tremendous experience.

I have always had a special admiration for this region of America. It has a quality all its own. In a few generations the people here built a civilization out of the desert.

There is no story in our history more typical of the free American spirit than that of the Mormon settlers who founded this great city. I have a close personal interest in the history of this great city. My grandfather, who lived in Jackson County, Missouri, was a freighter across the plains in the early days, and on occasion he brought an ox trainload of goods and merchandise here to Salt Lake City. My grandfather, whose name was Young, went to see Brigham Young and told him his troubles, and Brigham Young gave him advice and told him to rent space down on the main street here in Salt Lake City, place his goods on display, and he would guarantee that my grandfather would lose no money. And he didn't.

Today I am most cordially received by the president of the Mormon Church, the successor of Brigham Young. I wish my old grandfather could see me now!

Those pioneers had faith, and they had energy. They took the resources that Nature offered them and used them wisely. Their courage and fighting spirit made them secure against enemies.

They have left you a great heritage. You now have the responsibility for the wise use of the resources of this region. You now have the duty to protect your rights and your welfare against enemies who threaten them.

And these enemies do exist. Whether you know it or not, you are in battle against powerful forces that threaten your resources and your families and your hopes of the future. Tonight I am going to name these forces, so that you will all know whom we are fighting. First, let us see how this battle began.

You here in the West know a great deal about conserving natural resources, so that they will be useful to our children as well as to ourselves. You have learned by experience, and learned well.

What is the magic word in the prosperity of the farmers and the livestock men of this region? That word is "water." The first thing the Mormon settlers did, when they came here, after giving thanks to God for a safe arrival, was to dig irrigation ditches. They knew what they were doing. So long as you have water enough for farming and grazing, the basis of your welfare is assured.

I think it is no exaggeration to say that as the water goes, so goes this part of the country. Irrigation has given to the West a prosperous agriculture; it has brought thriving industries and enabled you to make use of your natural resources. With the aid of the government, you have built the great dams that provide you with water and hydroelectric power.

Water for irrigation and electric power for homes and farms and industries have gone hand in hand. It is fair to say that those who have helped you obtain the water and the power you need are your friends. And, by the same token, those who have hampered you in obtaining irrigation and electric power are your enemies; they are not your friends.

This is not a new battle. Selfish men have always tried to skim the cream from our natural resources to satisfy their own greed. And they have always sought to control the government in order to accomplish this. Their instrument in this effort has always been the Republican Party.

The Republican administrations of our time have done their best to make the West an economic colony of Wall Street. In the 1920s, under Harding, Coolidge, and Hoover, quick and greedy exploitation was the order of the day. Many parts of the West were withering — from the failure to develop its power and irrigation, withering actually from Republican sabotage.

Selfish men had control, and the great resources of the West were wasted with sinful disregard of the people. Never before in history had so much been wasted by so few. In some of the western states the population had actually begun to decline, reversing the historic progress of western expansion. Hope began to disappear.

That was the situation in 1932, after twelve years of Republican rule. At that time there were only twenty-eight reclamation projects in operation. Only three and a half million acres of land were under irrigation, and much of the irrigation was pitifully inadequate. Power plant capacity was very small. There was no comprehensive program to give the West access to its water resources. That was the Republican way with the West.

The people of the West cried out for a change — and finally, at long last, there came a change. The birthright of the West was finally restored to the people. It was restored by the Democratic Party under the leadership of Franklin D. Roosevelt.

The long, costly job of rebuilding after the ruinous Republican years was begun with hope and vigor. Conservation of the forests and grazing land, control of soil erosion, propagation of fish and wildlife, and other sound measures were put into effect. Development of the river basins was begun, with full attention to hydroelectric power and flood control.

Today, after four Democratic administrations, there are some sixty reclamation projects completed or under way in the West. When these projects are finished, they will provide water for over ten million acres and will produce over five million kilowatts of power. That's the record the Democratic Party has made. This record on western reclamation, the record of pledges made and kept, is one that Franklin Roosevelt was proud of — and I'm proud of that record too. As president, I shall never cease to fight for the public power and reclamation policies of the Democratic Party.

This is the time of year, every four years, when there are a lot of guessing games going on — guessing where some people stand. You have to guess, because some people won't come out in the open and tell you where they really stand.

Well, you don't have to do any guessing to know where the Democratic Party has stood for sixteen years on public power and reclamation — and where it stands today. And you don't have to translate any double-talk to know where I have always stood — and where I stand today.

I stand, and the Democratic Party stands, for rapid and uninterrupted development of the land and the forest and the water and the mineral resources of the West, in the interest of the people. I stand, and the Democratic Party stands, for building a strong western economy, based on full use of our natural resources and healthy development of industry. I stand for the rights of the people.

But where does the Republican Party stand? Where do its candidates stand? The record is clear enough for all of you to see.

In the first place, we all know that low-cost electric power is of tremendous importance to the West. Bonneville and Grand Coulee Dams brought about the establishment of a great aluminum industry in the Pacific Northwest.

A continuing increase in hydroelectric power could bring other great industries to the West. One of these is phosphate production. The West has enormous deposits of phosphate. Yet western farmers have to buy their phosphate fertilizer from processing plants two thousand miles away — and they have to pay the heavy cost of the long haul to the West. This comes to as much as $60 a ton more than farmers in the East have to pay. You have that prospect planned under any one of these great projects we are trying to build in the West.

It takes no great vision to see that phosphate fertilizer production is a natural industrial development for the West. All that is needed is a constant supply of low-cost electric power. Then what stands in the way of more hydroelectric power for the West? The answer is Republican policy. For the last two years, that Republican 80th Congress, listening obediently to the voice of its masters, has sabotaged industrial development of the West. And I want you to get this!

In 1947, at the first session of the 80th Congress, I requested an appropriation of $160 million as the minimum necessary for the work of reclamation to continue on an economical basis. Here was the first test of the attitude of the Republican leadership toward the West in fourteen years. The Republican-dominated House Appropriations Committee sliced nearly $90 million off my request.

When that happened, a great storm of protest arose over all the West. You made yourselves heard so loudly in Washington that you startled the Republican chairman of the House Appropriations Committee. "The West," he cried, "is squealing like a stuck pig."

There you have the Republican attitude toward the West summed up in a single phrase: "The West is squealing like a stuck pig." He squeals every time he has to make an appropriation in the public interest. The Republicans are ready to lead you to the slaughter, and they resent it if you protest.

This public pressure from the West eventually forced the reluctant 80th Congress to appropriate $104 million. But this sum was still more than $50 million short of the amount needed to keep the work of reclamation going forward continuously. Before the year ended, work on power and reclamation projects in the Columbia Basin and the Central Valley of California, on Davis Dam on the Lower Colorado, and on the Colorado–Big Thompson Project had to be sharply curtailed. On some big jobs, work had to stop.

At last, continued public pressure from the West — and constant pounding from me — compelled the Republican Congress to appropriate a supplemental amount in order to continue operations on these projects. They did it very reluctantly. That is the Republican way, the way by which the West would soon be "economized" once again into stagnation.

This year, to step up the construction program to meet the expanding needs of all the West, I requested an appropriation of almost $285 million for the reclamation program. That was the largest reclamation request in our history. I want you to understand that these are self-liquidating projects. They aren't giving you anything; they are merely advancing the money so that you can develop the country and pay it back.

The Republican 80th Congress realized that, in this election year, it had better pay some attention to the West. It finally approved an appropriation $40 million less than was needed to do the work. Even this appropriation was not aimed to benefit the people so much as to benefit the power interests.

While the Republican 80th Congress was considering this appropriation bill, highly paid lobbyists of the power interests poured into Washington. The influence of these agents of big business was plainly marked in the bill that passed the Congress. The Republican 80th Congress wrote into that bill some clauses that strike a dangerous blow at people in the West. Some of these clauses prohibit or slow down construction of new transmission lines and the extension of existing lines. You had better think that one over.

Ask yourselves a question: who benefits from the building of dams if the government does not also build transmission lines to carry the power from the dams to the people? Who benefits? The private power interests benefit, of course — at your expense! These interests, for years, have sought to force the government to sell them low-cost federal power in bulk at the dam — power which they could then sell to the people on their own terms.

The measures passed by the Republican 80th Congress will result in bigger profits for the private power companies and higher living costs for the people. Unless different action is taken in the next year, these measures will deprive consumers of cheaper power. They will deprive the government of power revenues from transmission and distribution — revenues which should be used to repay the costs of these power and reclamation projects.

This is a heavy and damaging blow to the development of the West. You have been crudely and wickedly cheated by the power lobby in Washington, operating through the Republican 80th Congress. The facts are plain. The private power monopoly, in the last two years of Republican congressional reaction, has fought the people. It has won a battle that threatens to cost the people of the West hundreds of millions of dollars for years ahead.

The record is clear. Under the Democrats, you will get imagination, initiative, and progress. Under the Republicans, you get strangulation. You have a clear-cut choice in the election on November the 2nd.

The Republican Party has shown in the Congress of the past two years that the leopard does not change his spots. It is still the party of Harding, Coolidge, and Hoover. It is still the party that gave you the phony Coolidge boom and the Hoover depression. It is still the party whose money at election time comes from Wall Street. It is still the party which passes bills at the dictation of lobbies, and sacrifices the interests of the people for the profits of big business.

The Democratic Party is the party of the people. We are fighting with all our strength to prevent the gluttons of privilege from swallowing up the country. We are fighting the battle of the West, because it is the battle of all the country. We are fighting the battle of the farmer and the worker and the small businessman, because that is the battle of all the people.

Your government is now planning the most ambitious irrigation development in all our history. The goal of our program is to bring every possible western acre under irrigation and to develop to the fullest extent the hydroelectric resources of this great region. Now, I'm going to fight for this program with all I've got. Now, can I count on you? You have the decision to make. A vote for the Republicans stops the program. A vote for the Democrats is a vote for a glorious West with wealth and security for our people.

On election day, the plain people of the country need to roll up a wide tide of votes that will sweep the forces of fear and reaction out of the government and open the gates again for hope and progress. We must go forward together, toward the fulfillment of our American destiny — the use of all our resources for all our people.

NOTE: In his opening words the president referred to Herbert B. Maw, governor of Utah, and George A. Smith, president of the Church of Jesus Christ of Latter-day Saints.

SEPTEMBER 23

Rear Platform Remarks

Fresno, California (8:12 A.M.)

Mr. Chairman, Congressman White, and citizens of the great Central Valley of California:

It has been a very great pleasure to me to receive the welcome which I have received in this part of the world. I believe you are interested in the welfare of the country as a whole, as well as in the welfare in California, when you turn out like this to see the president.

I was supposed to get up at 4:00 this morning for a bunch of people up here in Tracy at 5:00, but I didn't make it! I was sorry about that, but then you know, a workhorse can do only so many hours in a day, and I skipped that one.

I was up at the next stop, though, to see them at 6:00 and 6:45 and now at 8; and I think everybody who was at those other stops is here too — or else this great city of Fresno is much bigger than I thought it was.

You are interested in the agricultural welfare of this nation more than any other one thing. Your interests are diversified, and a diversified farming community can only be prosperous when the government of the United States is interested in the welfare of the farmer.

I can remember very well, I ran a farm for the best ten years of my life in Jackson County, Missouri. It had six hundred acres on it, and I went there when I was twenty-two years old and left it when I was thirty-three to go to war. I didn't claim any exemption on account of that farm, nor did I claim my exemption for being thirty-three years old. I went over and joined a battery of field artillery. There are a few fellows on this train who have been with me in that division. I am not bragging about that, because that is just what I ought to have done, but I wanted to impress upon you that I know something about the farm situation.

In that day and age we had no federal government interested in the farmer. Along in the 1920s they became less interested in the farmer, and if I remember correctly, in 1932 there were 123,000 farmers kicked off their farms. Do you know how many were kicked off their farms last year who couldn't pay their debts? Just 800! That's some difference — that's some difference!

Do you know what caused that difference? Because the government of the United States became interested in the farmer and the workingman and the white-collar man and the little businessman.

Well, along in 1946 the farmers were all fat and rich, and had money in the bank, and they turned almost economic royalists and they didn't go and vote. That let this country become entangled under this Republican 80th "do-nothing" Congress. The first thing that happened to them — that Congress began immediately to cut the ground from under the farmer, and they have almost succeeded in doing it. They have made it impossible for the Commodity Credit Corporation to furnish storage for those crops under the support price, and that was done with malice aforethought, because that Republican Congress does not believe in price support.

I wonder where you raisin fellows would be out here in the valley if it weren't for the farm policy of the Democratic Party! I wonder where you cotton fellows would be if it weren't for the price support policy of the United States government? Here's a cotton man right here — he can tell you something about that.

Now, you want to analyze this situation carefully and thoroughly. I am not asking you to vote for me alone. I want you to vote for yourselves. Vote for your own interests. Vote for the interests of the whole country.

Of course, if you are not interested in the interests of the whole country, then vote for these economic royalists and let them take you over. That is what they hope to do. This Republican 80th Congress is only the first step. It doesn't make any difference what they say they believe. Actions speak louder than words. What you need to do is understand what this 80th Congress did to the farmer and the laboring man and the white-collar worker, and you can't help but make your mind up in the right direction.

Now, on November the 2nd I want you to get up and work just as hard to win this election for the party that is for the people as you have worked this morning to get here to look at the president of the United States. While you are doing that, elect Mr. White to the Congress. You have got a terrible congressman here in this district. He is one of the worst. He is one of the worst obstructionists in the Congress. He has done everything he possibly could to cut the throats of the farmer and the laboring man. If you send him back, that will be your fault if you get your own throat cut.

I am speaking plainly these days. I am telling you facts. Nobody else will tell 'em to you.

If you will just sit down and analyze this situation, you can't do but one thing, and that is send the Democrats into power in Washington for the next four years.

It is a great pleasure and a privilege for me to come out here and talk to you people and tell you just what I believe in. I have made it perfectly plain in Des Moines what my program is with regard to the farmer. I made it perfectly plain in Detroit what my program is in regard to the workingman. And they don't clash. The prosperity of the farmer and the workingman march side by side. When one is prosperous, the other is. When one is not prosperous, the other is not prosperous, and he is out of a job. I told them at Salt Lake City just where I stand on conservation and public power, and I also reiterated that last night at Oakland, California.

You don't have to worry about where I stand. You know! I want you to see whether you can find out where the opposition stands. I'll bet you can't.

NOTE: The president referred to Cecil F. White, Democratic candidate for Congress.

SEPTEMBER 23

Address at the Gilmore Stadium

Los Angeles (9:30 P.M.)

Mr. Chairman, and ladies and gentlemen:

I have come here tonight to tell you where I stand on the big issues before the country in this campaign.

This is a championship fight. And I am convinced of one thing: the American people are sold on the idea that nobody deserves to win a championship fight by running away. I do not believe that anybody is going to win this fight by running away from the record or ducking the issues.

In our system, the people have a right to know exactly what our two major parties stand for on specific issues. They have a right to know who is for them and who is against them.

The decisive battle has arrived. The people are going to have to choose one side or the other. The Democratic Party and I have nothing to conceal. We are proud of our record. The underlying struggle in this campaign is a struggle between two sets of ideals.

The Democratic ideal of America is summed up in the four freedoms:

freedom from want, freedom from fear, freedom of worship, and freedom of speech. The Republican ideal, as I have seen it in action, is summed up in one phrase: "Big business first."

Today, I regret to say, certain great business interests are trying to corrupt the American idealism. With the Republican Party as their instrument, they are waging a war against the aspirations of our people.

These shrewd men aim to take advantage of the prosperity which you have attained in the last few years with Democratic government. They know that in the throes of prosperity, voters are not easily excited. They hope that this year a large number of voters will not bother to go to the polls. That is their only chance of winning. Some of their franker spokesmen have said in so many words that they are counting on a light vote on election day.

With that in mind, they are trying their best to avoid any suggestion that there is something to fight about in this campaign. They are trying to lull you to sleep with "high-level" platitudes. They are saying in effect: "Everything is all right, everything will go on being all right, if you will just forget about politics and leave things to us."

I wish from the bottom of my heart that that were true. I wish from the heart that it were possible to say to the American people, with sincerity, that it does not make any difference which party they elect this year, that everything will be all right no matter what happens.

But that is not true. As president of the United States, I know that everything will not be all right, unless the American people exercise care and vigilance to keep the gains which they have won. These past two years have shown us evidence — frightening evidence — that if the country falls into the hands of the leaders of the Republican Party, everything is likely to be all wrong within a very short time.

We in this country know how abruptly conditions can change. Just twenty years ago the Republicans were assuring us that everything was going to be all right. But a few months later everything was all wrong. And everything stayed all wrong until the American public elected Franklin D. Roosevelt.

No one can deny that this country has benefited from Democratic administrations. It is the Democratic Party that has been working for the people for the past sixteen years and getting results for them. It is the Democratic Party that ended discouragement and fear under the Republicans and opened the gate to a new era of prosperity in this country.

Farmers, workers, homeowners, small businessmen — every American has reason to remember the constructive work of the Democratic administrations since 1933: Social Security, the farm program, collective bargaining, the minimum wage law, slum clearance, low-rent housing, TVA, soil conservation, reclamation and irrigation projects, full employment, world leadership, the highest standards of living in the history of the world. You can sum up in these few words an era of progress with Democratic administrations which believed in the people and worked for the people.

But these are things that happened in the past. And you and I, and all of us, are concerned with what is happening now and what will happen in the days immediately ahead.

I don't expect the American people to vote my way just because the Democratic Party served them well after the Republican Party had let them down. But I do expect the American people to wake up and realize right now, this very instant, their standard of living and their hopes for the future are at stake.

I'm not going to use high-sounding words. I speak plainly and directly. I am going to use hard facts. The people of California and of the entire nation are entitled to the facts.

We'll start with some hard facts about housing. This is a great and growing city. People are pouring into it every day. But the supply of houses is pitifully inadequate. Why? The real estate lobby and the Republican Party in Congress have seen to that. Eight years ago, only 5 percent of the houses sold in Los Angeles cost under $3,500. Today only 1 out of 30 sells for so little — if you can find it. Eight years ago, only 5 percent of the houses sold in Los Angeles cost over $10,000. Today 50 percent cost over $10,000 — again, if you have one, if you have the $10,000 and can find the house. Many people can't find a house at any price. Many are doubling up with the other families. Thousands of citizens in this city are forced to live in trailers and unsanitary shacks.

The Democratic administration knows that not all families can afford to buy their own houses at a price that yields a profit to the bankers and builders. We know that many families, particularly young veterans, need low-rent housing, which requires federal support.

Almost three years ago, after long and exhaustive study, the Wagner-Ellender-Taft Housing Bill was introduced in the Congress. This represented a long-range program to provide the fifteen million new homes we shall need. Among other things, it provided for slum clearance, rural housing, and low-rent housing projects.

Time and again I urged the passage of that bill. But it was opposed by a million-dollar real estate lobby in Washington. It passed the Senate, only to be killed in the House of Representatives. Last year the same bill was introduced again. Again it passed the Senate. It was murdered by the Republican leadership in the House of Representatives, by some of the ugliest trickery in the history of the Congress.

Last July, because the need for housing was so desperate, I called a special session of the 80th Congress. Since the Republican National Convention had specifically endorsed slum clearance and low-rent housing in its platform, I hoped that we could finally get some action.

But the real estate lobby was still at work, and again the Republican Congress obeyed the voice of its masters. The House Republicans blocked the bill. The Republican head of a powerful committee in the House used his power to refuse to let the House of Representatives vote on public housing.

The fight went into the Senate. What happened there? Senator Taft of Ohio, who had helped to sponsor the original measure, actually took the lead in fighting his own bill and voted against it. By their votes ye shall know them!

These are hard facts. These facts tell you as plain as day what Republican leaders are doing to you right now and what they will do to you ten times over if they get full control of your government. These facts tell you, too, how little faith you can have in Republican platform promises and campaign promises.

Let's look at some more hard facts. Facts about Social Security, for example. In 1944 the Republican Party spoke out boldly for extending Social Security. That was a fine platform promise. But what happened? The Republican 80th Congress actually passed a law, not to extend Social Security, but to take Social Security away from hundreds of thousands of American workers. That's the way they kept their promises. I vetoed this measure. Ninety-eight percent of the Republicans in Congress voted to override my veto.

Let's look at the facts about health legislation. You know how hard it is to find a room in a hospital. You know how hard it is to pay the bills when sickness hits your family.

We worked out a painstaking plan for national medical care. It was designed to meet the medical needs of the American people. It provided for new hospitals, clinics, health centers, research, and a system of national health insurance. Who opposed it? The well-organized medical lobby. Who killed it? The Republican 80th "do-nothing" Congress.

After the Republicans had killed the bill as a whole, we still tried to pass parts of it. The Republican Party in Congress had become a little uneasy by that time. They were not quite sure how the people would like what they were doing. So they tried to make their record on health legislation look a little better. They passed a dental research bill. But having done that, they failed to provide any money to carry it out.

Then these Republican so-called representatives of the people passed a bill to conduct research in heart disease. That's an important thing for this country, for as you know, heart disease is on the increase. On the basis of the best advice, I recommended nearly $7 million as the minimum requirement. But the Republican Congress cut the appropriation to a mere half-million dollars, only one-fourteenth of what was needed.

Everywhere you look, it's the same story. I asked for aid to education for the benefit of the children of this country. No action by the Republican 80th Congress. I asked for a curb on inflation. No action by the Republican Congress.

The story of the fight on inflation is especially revealing. When I called the Congress into special session this summer, I urged it to deal with the high cost of living. The Republican leadership replied that this was a political maneuver on my part in an election year.

Let's nail that one right now. The Republicans know perfectly well that I had previously called a special session of the Republican 80th Congress in November 1947 to deal with inflation and the high cost of living. And 1947 was not an election year. When I called the special session for the same purpose in 1948, it was because the Congress had failed to act for the preceding year and a half.

The dangers of inflation are continuing to grow. The cost of living is continuing to rise. The Republicans cannot conceal their responsibility by hurling charges of "politics" at me. There is no great mystery about how to stop the cost of living from going higher and higher. The best way to stop it is with price control. Everybody knows that when we had price control, the average family was not gouged by inflated prices. Everybody knows that rents under price control have not skyrocketed. But meat and other foods and automobiles and building materials, without price control, have gone up and up and up.

These are the facts. I have been urging price control, because it is a realistic way, a tested way, of holding down the cost of living. A program that does not include price control will not, and cannot, hold down the cost of living. We have learned that from hard experience.

Instead of dealing vigorously with inflation, the Republican leadership preferred to try to make a political issue of it. They blame government expenditures for the rising cost of living. The fact is that the government expenditures were vastly greater during the war than they are now, and yet we stabilized the cost of living. During the war we shipped far more goods and supplies overseas than we are shipping now, and yet we stabilized the cost of living.

These are the hard facts that you voters will want to bear in mind when you go to the polls on election day. These are the facts that make this election a decisive battle in the life of our country. These are the facts which show that this is a critical struggle between the forward forces of liberalism and the backward forces of reaction.

While I am talking about the forces of progressive liberalism, I want to add a word to all the people of California who believe in liberal ideas. You, like Americans everywhere today, are disturbed about the threat to peace and the failures of the 80th Congress to deal with basic economic problems here at home. Most of the people realize that the Democratic administration is doing everything that can be done to preserve the peace. And they realize that the Democratic administration is eager to put an end to the reactionary policies of the 80th Congress.

There are, however, some people with true liberal convictions whose worry over the state of the world has caused them to lean toward a third party. To these liberals I would say in all sincerity: think again.

The fact that the Communists are guiding and using the third party shows that this party does not represent American ideals. But there is another and very practical reason why it is folly for any liberal to put his hope in this third party. The third party has no power in the government and no chance of achieving power. The simple fact is that the third party cannot achieve peace, because it is powerless. It cannot achieve better conditions here at home, because it is powerless.

The Democratic Party is the party which truly expresses the hopes of American liberals and which has power to fulfill those hopes. We have worked for peace in a difficult international situation, and we shall continue with all our strength to work for peace. We have worked for the improvement of the conditions here at home — to curb inflation, to provide low-rent housing, give aid to education, extend civil rights, and scores of other ways. I shall continue to work for these goals with all my strength.

A vote for the third party can only weaken the efforts of the Democratic

Party to build a healthy nation and a peaceful world. A vote for the third party plays into the hands of the Republican forces of reaction, whose aims are directly opposed to the aims of American liberalism. A vote for the third party will not promote the cause of American liberalism; it will injure it. I say to those disturbed liberals who have been sitting uncertainly on the outskirts of the third party: think again. Don't waste your vote.

This is the hour for the liberal forces of America to unite. We have hopes to fulfill and goals to attain. Together we can rout the forces of reaction once again. We are strong in faith and strong in energy. We must entrust our destiny to those who will safeguard our rights, our freedom, and our national honor.

NOTE: The president's opening words "Mr. Chairman" referred to state senator George Luckey, vice chairman of the California State Democratic Committee.

SEPTEMBER 27

Address at the Bonham High School Football Stadium
Bonham, Texas (8:40 P.M.)

Speaker Rayburn — I say that advisedly — Governor Jester, Governor Turner of Oklahoma, and distinguished guests:

I have a warm spot in my heart for Texas. Texas has given me some of the best friends a man ever had, and a great many of them are on this platform with me tonight. There's John Myer and Wright Patman and Lyndon Johnson — candidates for Congress in the great state of Texas who are real men and who have always been for the people first. And then you have nominated a man for the Senate, my good friend and the friend of the people of Texas, Lyndon Johnson.

The people of Oklahoma have nominated my good friend, Bob Kerr, for the Senate in Oklahoma, and if Lyndon Johnson and Bob Kerr get to the Senate, we'll make those Republicans dance in the next session.

I am more than happy to be here today in the hometown of one of the finest and best friends of them all — Sam Rayburn. I understand that Sam asked you folks to come out here today so we could talk a little politics. I'm glad so many of you came, because it shows that you're interested in your

House Democratic leader Sam Rayburn, whose party would recapture a majority in the 1948 election, was among Truman's closest friends. (Chicago Sun-Times)

government — and interested in the kind of government you're going to have after the election next November.

One thing is certain. In Texas it's going to be Democratic government, as it has been in the past; and that's a good way to keep it, because the Democratic Party is the party that works for the people.

So far as the federal government is concerned, the Republicans are putting on an immense propaganda campaign in an effort to take over this year. They are spending tremendous sums of money and lining up all kinds of strange bedfellows.

I just don't believe they're going to get away with it. We Democrats are going to see that the American people know the facts. When they do, I don't think the people will be taken in by slick Republican propaganda. I don't believe that Texas — or the rest of the United States — wants to go back to the days of Harding, Coolidge, and Hoover.

The country will make a fundamental decision on election day — a decision which will affect you every year and every day for the rest of your lives. The people will have to decide between the Democratic and the Republican parties; and that is really a decision between two different kinds of government.

The Democratic Party will give you the kind of government that Sam Rayburn stands for — government in the interest of the farmer and the workingman and all the people. And when the Democrats have a majority in the House of Representatives, Sam Rayburn will have a powerful voice in seeing that you get the kind of government you ought to have.

Some people have wondered why I keep on talking about the Republican 80th "do-nothing" Congress. Well, I'll tell you why. It's because they raised a storm warning that tells us what we could expect if we had a Republican president as well as a Republican Congress. We might have "unity" then. I don't know. But if we did have unity, what kind would it be?

Well, it would be the unity of the Martins and the Tabers and the Wherrys and the Tafts. Then it would be unity in giving tax relief to the rich at the expense of the poor, unity in refusing to give aid to our schools, unity in letting prices go sky-high in order to protect excessive profits, unity in whittling away all the benefits of the New Deal, about which the Republicans are so scornful. But they have never yet offered to repeal any of the New Deal measures that were put on the books in the last sixteen years.

Do you want that kind of unity? Do you want that kind of unity? Well, I don't either.

Some things are worth fighting for. We have to fight the special-interest lobbies instead of being "unified" by them. We must fight isolationists and reactionaries, the profiteers and the privileged class.

The way to fight it is to fight them with votes. When the people know the leaders of the Republican Party are tied up with big business and the special interests, then the people will know how to deal with them at the polls.

That is why I keep talking about these Republicans in the 80th Congress and what they did to the people. Part of the story is of special concern to the Texas farmer, although it affects every American. That is the attitude of the Republican Party toward international trade. The 80th Congress has shown that the Republican Party is still a high-tariff party of Smoot and Hawley and Joe Grundy. And you can't expect anyone under an obligation to Joe Grundy to change it into some other kind of party.

When Cordell Hull wrote the reciprocal trade agreements program which came up for renewal this year, the Republicans in Congress insisted on a lot of crippling amendments. Moreover, they renewed it for only one year instead of the usual three. And now, apparently, they wanted to be in a position to do something next year that they didn't dare do this year, because this year is an election year. It's obvious what they want to do next year. They just want to kill the program entirely.

This is a matter of concern to every man, woman, and child in the United States because it vitally affects our prospects for world peace. A thriving world trade is essential to world prosperity. And prosperity is fundamental to peace and security.

When a man gets too hungry, he gets desperate. Just the same way with nations. Poverty and distress breed war. Foreign trade is not merely a way to keep prosperity. It is the best way to ensure peace.

Your government is making every effort to establish a just and permanent peace. That has always been the main objective of my administration. For that purpose the Democratic administration established a bipartisan foreign policy, taking the Republican Party into our confidence and working with them in matters concerning our relations with other countries.

One of the great architects of our foreign policy, as you know, is your own Senator Tom Connally. From the beginning Tom Connally has contributed a full measure of hard work and statesmanship in making the policy work.

The bipartisan foreign policy has added greatly to the strength of our efforts for peace. But the peace can be no more secure than the foundations upon which it rests. And if the Republican Party will not join us in establishing a firm basis for world trade, the foundation of peace will be very shaky indeed.

Vigorous world trade is necessary to maintain our domestic prosperity. The farmers of Texas know the truth of that statement from the hard lesson of experience. They know that adequate foreign markets help to provide stable farm incomes. They know that barriers to foreign trade mean farm depression.

Let me give you an illustration. During World War I, American wheat growers expanded their production to meet the great foreign demand for wheat. Shortly after that war, the foreign markets dried up, and the wheat farmers were left high and dry. You know what happened to prices — they kept falling until finally many farmers were selling wheat for 25 cents a bushel.

The same thing happened to cotton. The Republican high tariffs and trade barriers put up after the First World War cut down the trade in cotton and put the cotton prices on the skids. Farmers were finally selling cotton for 5 cents a pound. You know that the Republicans who were then in office did absolutely nothing about it.

Now we are faced with problems like those that followed the First World War. This year we are producing bumper crops of cotton and grain. We mean to keep producing big crops.

The world needs our crops, and our farmers want to sell them. Other countries want to sell their products to the United States to pay for what they buy. And we in the United States need the products they want to sell.

The Democratic administration has been doing a great deal to protect the export markets for your crops. I have spoken of the Reciprocal Trade Agreements. Also, your government has taken the lead in setting up the International Trade Organization.

In addition we negotiated a special international agreement relating to wheat. The practical effect of the International Wheat Agreement would have been just this. Now, listen carefully. Our farmers would have had guaranteed markets, domestic and foreign, for billion-bushel wheat crops for a minimum of five years, at prices at least as good as those assured by our price support program.

The wheat agreement was submitted to the United States Senate to be ratified as a treaty. What happened to it? The Republican leadership of the Senate wouldn't even allow it to be brought up on the floor of the Senate for consideration. The Republicans killed the International Wheat Agreement.

That is how they love the farmers. This is the kind of treatment the farmer has been getting from the Republican Party, and that's the kind of treatment he can expect to keep on getting from that party. Don't you forget that, now, on election day.

Look at what they have been saying about cotton. The Republican press has been having a field day warning people that the government may have to make a lot of cotton loans this year at a rate of around 30 cents a pound. They talk as if that is a bad thing to do. They use it as an argument against the whole support price program.

They don't tell you how cotton loans rescued the farmer from the mess of 1932 or how useful government stocks were during World War II. They don't tell you that the Truman administration set up a vigorous cotton export program at the end of the war and completely wiped out the last of the cotton surplus — the headache that had plagued farmers for a quarter of a century.

Yes, and we've still got a vigorous cotton export policy. Sam Rayburn can tell you about the $150 million revolving fund that he finally pushed through a reluctant Congress in June. That fund will help us keep on using American cotton in the occupied areas of Germany and Japan.

As long as I have anything to say about it, we'll keep on knocking down trade barriers and opening up foreign markets for American cotton. And we will drive just as hard to hold and expand the home market, by improving the product, finding new uses, and cutting costs of production.

The Republicans tell you not to worry, while they threaten the Reciprocal Trade Agreements, not to worry while they refuse international cooperation through a wheat agreement, and not to worry while they attack your price supports. This shows very clearly the real principle of the Republican Party. That is the "trickle-down" principle. Take care of the big boys and some money will trickle down to the little fellow.

That's just opposite of the Democratic way. Our primary concern is for the little fellow. We think the big boys have always done very well, taking care of themselves, and they will always take care of themselves. It is the business of the government to see that the little fellow gets a square deal.

As a matter of fact, I have nothing against the big boys until they get in the way of progress. You sometimes find one who wants the little fellow to get a break. But that is very seldom; you don't find them very often.

Ask Sam Rayburn how many of the big-money boys helped when he was sweating blood to get electricity for farmers and the people in the small towns. You know, Sam was one of the fathers of the Rural Electrification Administration. It's a great monument to him.

When he started working to get REA, you folks in Texas had electricity on very few farms — only on twenty-three farms in every thousand. Last year, over half of the farms in Texas had electricity. And we intend to push that program vigorously during the next four years. That's an example of what I mean, when I say that the Democratic Party works for the people. And in this case, as in so many others, the Democratic Party did it over violent Republican opposition.

There have been six record votes in Congress on REA. In all but one of those record votes, only about 12 to 25 percent of the Republicans voted in favor of the REA. The vast majority of Republicans opposed REA, and the vast majority of Democrats supported it. The REA program owes its birth and its present life and vigor to the Democratic Party.

I am deeply concerned about what the Republicans would do to the Rural Electrification Program if they could get control of the whole government. I know that the Republican 80th Congress was not willing to bring low-cost electric power to consumers that would stand in the way of the profits of the private power monopolies. And that power monopoly had one of the most powerful lobbies in Washington that ever came there.

I could go on and on about Republican failures. They've made enough mistakes to give me ammunition to talk from now to Christmas. But I don't want to wear out my welcome in Texas. After all, nothing I could say about the Republicans is half as bad as their record. In fact, it is because the Republican record is so bad that I am sure the Democrats will win this election.

I have a profound faith in the people of this country. I believe in their common sense. They love freedom, and that love for freedom and justice is not dead.

Our people believe today, as Jefferson did, that men were not born with saddles on their backs to be ridden by the privileged few. We believe, as Jefferson did, that "God who gave us life gave us liberty." We protect our liberty against those who threaten it from abroad, and we do not propose to give it up to those who threaten it at home. We will not give up our democratic way to a dictatorship of the left; neither will we give it up to a despotism of special privilege.

The people of this congressional district have shown that they share these convictions. They have shown it by sending Sam Rayburn to Congress time after time. And when I go down to the Capitol to address the Congress next January, I expect to see Sam Rayburn sitting up in the Speaker's chair where he belongs.

Thank you very much.

NOTE: In his opening words the president referred to Representative Sam Rayburn of Texas, Governor Beauford H. Jester of Texas, and Governor Roy J. Turner of Oklahoma. Later he referred to Representatives Wright Patman and Lyndon B. Johnson, Democratic candidate for senator, both of Texas; Robert S. Kerr, Democratic candidate for senator from Oklahoma; Joseph R. Grundy, former senator from Pennsylvania; and Tom Connally, senator from Texas. Truman also referred to House Speaker Joseph Martin of Massachusetts, House Appropriations Committee chairman John Taber of New York, and Senators Kenneth Wherry of Nebraska and Robert A. Taft of Ohio. He also made reference to former senator Reed Smoot of Utah, former congressman Willis Hawley of Oregon, and Pennsylvania Republican leader Joseph Grundy.

OCTOBER 8

Address at Eagles Hall
Buffalo (10:05 P.M.)

Mr. Chairman:

In less than a month, you will have the responsibility of choosing a government for the next four years, 1949 to 1953.

These are likely to be critical years in American history, and in world history. They are years which are likely to hold the answer to two great questions in the hearts of most of us today. These questions I can briefly sum up as (1) war or peace? (2) hard times or prosperity?

Now, as to the first question, war or peace. I know that every right-thinking American wants peace. I believe that our prayers will be answered and that we will have peace. No one wants peace in the world more than I do. I have said time and again that I would rather have peace in the world than to be president of the United States.

Of course, present world conditions are of grave concern to all of us. Because of these conditions, I have found it necessary to cancel visits I had planned to make to a number of cities tomorrow. I must return to Washington to meet with Secretary of State Marshall, who is flying back from Paris to confer with me. I shall discuss with Secretary Marshall means for working out constructive and peaceful solutions to our problems abroad, within the framework of our basic American principles and within the framework of the United Nations.

I am sorry to disappoint so many of my friends whom I had expected to see tomorrow. But I know that they will forgive me.

Now, tonight I am going to talk to you about the second great question I mentioned — hard times or prosperity. The election in November clearly presents that question to the people of the United States.

Of course, there is no open argument on this question. Nobody wants hard times. Everybody wants prosperity. The Republicans are quite sincere in saying that they want prosperity just as much as the Democrats. I believe they do. Who doesn't?

But the leaders who now control the Republican Party want prosperity for special-privilege groups first, and for other people if they can get it. They want high profits of their campaign contributors and high prices for special-interest lobbies.

In the mad scramble to get that selfish kind of prosperity, they forget about the rest of the country. They forget about the needs of the farmer and labor and small business. They forget about housewives struggling with their budgets, and families using up their savings to meet the high cost of living. They forget about the prosperity of the consumers and wage earners of this country. Then, of course their own prosperity goes to smash under those circumstances, and they are all in depression together.

Real prosperity is based on justice. Real prosperity depends on fair treatment for all groups of our society. That's a rule as old as the Bible. That's what the Bible means when it says, and I quote: "We are . . . every one members, one of another." That is the very thing the economists have found out about our economy, after fifty years of studying booms and depressions.

We judge people and parties by what they do, not by what they say. We judge the Democratic Party by its record of achievement over the last sixteen years. We judge the Republican Party by its record of the last two years in the Congress, where it has had absolute control of the legislative branch of the government, and complete responsibility for that branch.

If we look at that record, we can see that the Republican leadership had changed very little in its policies since the days of Hoover. And we can see that the Republican Party is following the same fatal course — privileges for the few, neglect of the many — that led us into the disaster of 1929.

I know that this kind of talk is very painful to Republican leaders. I can't help that. The Republicans say I ought not to talk about the past. They would like us to forget the period from 1929 to 1932. They would like to forget it themselves, I am sure.

Let me assure you that when I talk about the Republican past, I do so with regret. I wish with all my heart that the Republican Party no longer had anything in common with the party that produced the depression of the 1930s.

But it is important for the people of this country to recognize that time has not changed the fundamental outlook of the Republican Party since it was last in power. The leopard has not changed his spots; he has merely hired some public relations experts. They have taught him to wear sheep's clothing and to purr sweet nothings about unity in a soothing voice. But it's the same old leopard.

The Republican strategy in this campaign is increasingly clear. The Republicans have carefully appraised their assets and liabilities and have reached the conclusion that they have one main liability and one main asset.

The liability is the issues in this campaign. They have concluded that their record is so bad on the important issues of the day that they can't even discuss them. The problems that affect the welfare of every person in this country are completely ignored by the Republican orators.

Now, the main asset of the Republicans is the tremendous financial support they are receiving. Much of it is being utilized to conduct a widespread propaganda campaign designed to fool you into believing that the result of this coming election is a foregone conclusion. How wrong they are!

I believe that the American people will not be fooled by this insidious propaganda. I believe that the American people — and not the propagandists for special interests — will decide in whose hands their government will be placed.

Now let us look at some of the issues in this campaign.

I do not claim that all Democrats are perfect or that all Democratic congressmen are wise. But in general, most Democrats vote for the people, and most Republicans vote for special interests. Just take, as an example, my proposals for the control of high prices. In 1947, in the Senate, 90 percent of the Democrats voted for these proposals, and 10 percent of the Democrats against them; but only 5 percent of the Republicans voted for them, and

95 percent of the Republicans voted against those proposals. In 1948, 81 percent of the Democrats voted for these proposals to hold prices down, and 98 percent of the Republicans voted against them.

I want you to realize that when I speak of the actions of the Republican 80th Congress, I am speaking of actions which represent the prevailing views of those who control the Republican Party. That Congress was merely a symbol and instrument of Republican Party policy.

Lately there has been talk by Republicans that while the 80th Congress might have been pretty bad — and I say it is more than pretty bad — that has nothing to do with the Republican leaders. They are attempting to build up the illusion that a Republican Congress and the Republican candidate for president do not stand for the same policies. Can you beat that?

Well, the Republican candidate has now dispelled that illusion. He has endorsed the 80th Congress. He said, and I quote: "The 80th Congress delivered as no other Congress ever did for the future of the country." How they delivered!

Make no mistake: when we talk of the failures of the 80th congress, we are talking of the policies of the Republican candidates, as well as most of the Republican congressmen and senators. They are tarred with the same brush — that brush that big business used to brush off the needs and the claims of the people.

Now, the point I want to drive home to you and to all the people of the United States is this: your prosperity is endangered by the Republican policies. I want you to look at the facts, think about them, and be guided by them.

And I am not asking you to vote for the Democratic Party just because during the past sixteen years Democratic policies turned hard times into good times. What I want you to do is to look at the present Democratic policies, as they affect you and your family in the years ahead.

Let's take a specific example. Let's take the struggle to get sufficient housing in this country. This year, in the United States of America, five million families are living in slums and fire traps. Another four million families are living in houses that will soon become slums unless something is done to prevent it. Three million families, including many families of war veterans, are living doubled up with other families. And things are getting worse. There are twice as many couples getting married each year as there are homes being built.

The housing situation is intolerable and inexcusable. A great, rich country like ours can afford decent homes for its citizens. We must do three things: we must build more houses, we must build homes that people — particularly young people — can afford, and we must clear out and rebuild the slums.

Houses are being built — by private enterprise, and they should be. But they aren't being built in sufficient numbers or at low enough prices. And without government help, they can't be. Without government help, cities are not financially able to wipe out their slums. So the government has a big and important role to play in housing, not in conflict or competition with private enterprise but supplementing it.

In my postwar message to the Congress, I urged early action by the Congress to enact a real housing program to meet these needs. That was in September 1945 — three years ago. My Message on the State of the Union, September 26, with twenty-one points in it, had one on housing.

A splendid bill for this purpose was introduced. It was sponsored by two Democrat Senators and one Republican. One of the Democrats was your own fighting, great liberal — Bob Wagner. The other Democratic senator was Senator Ellender of Louisiana, and the Republican was Senator Taft of Ohio.

I was hopeful that we could start helping our people with their housing problems. But I did not reckon with the influence of the real estate lobby. The real estate people have one of the most powerful, best organized, and most brazen lobbies in Washington. And the Republican Party has proved to be its faithful servant. The Wagner-Ellender-Taft bill passed the Senate in 1946 but was blocked by the Republican members of a House committee in the House of Representatives.

In 1947 we had the Republican 80th Congress — and you got that by staying at home and not doing your duty — and the housing bill was introduced again. The Republican leadership in the Senate stalled for time. Do you know what they did? They set up a joint committee to find out if there was a housing shortage.

I sent a message to Congress, asking them please to hurry up and do something. Housing conditions were getting worse and worse and are getting worse and worse. Thereupon, the Senate passed the bill for a second time, and it went to the House. There were enough favorable votes in the House to pass it, if it ever came to a vote. So the Republican leadership decided to keep it from coming to a vote. They pulled every trick in the parliamentary book, and some that had never been heard of before; and they were successful in keeping that housing bill from passing. It was a most shameful performance.

The Democrats tried again and again, in both the Senate and House, to get that bill through. But they were blocked at every turn by the Republicans. And the sad truth is that the Republican leadership in the Congress murdered that housing bill.

Congress adjourned shortly after that, and the Republicans went to their convention in Philadelphia, and they drafted a platform plank on housing. And what do you think that plank said? Don't be surprised now. It announced the stern determination of the Republican Party to provide federal housing aid for local slum clearance and low-rent housing programs — the very provisions they have been fighting against so hard for three years.

Beat that, if you can! That wasn't all the tommyrot they put in that platform — they put a lot of things in that platform that they had been fighting me on ever since I came to the presidency.

And then I got a glimmer of hope — not much, but a little. I thought they really wouldn't dare go back on their own platform — at least, not until the ink was dry on it — and that they might now pass the legislation they promised to the people. And I called them into special session, you remember, when I made that acceptance speech at the Democratic National Convention.

Well, you remember what happened. I called the Congress back into special session. I pointed out that unless it acted on housing, the next Congress would have to begin all over again and there would be another year's delay. I asked the Congress again to pass the Taft-Ellender-Wagner bill. You see, they turned it around. In the beginning it was the Wagner-Ellender-Taft bill, and they turned it around and called it the Taft-Ellender-Wagner bill.

Were the Republicans grateful for the chance to prove they meant what they said? Not a bit! They accused me of playing politics.

Now, we come to the end of this sorry story of Republican trickery. Senator Taft himself — one of the sponsors of the bill — turned against it and asked the Senate to kill it, to kill his own bill. Also very interesting is the fact that one of your senators from New York — who is close to the Republican candidate for president — had the chance to take a position on the housing bill. And Senator Ives voted against the bill.

So the Senate killed the Taft-Ellender-Wagner bill, and the Congress passed a bill, which does nothing about low-cost public housing, nothing about slum clearance, nothing about rural housing — nothing, in short, that they said they would do for the people in their platform.

One of the aims of my administration has been to give all our people a chance to have decent housing. Our major effort has been to enlarge the effective field of private enterprise and to give public support only to housing for those low-income families that private enterprise cannot serve. The Republican Congress flatly refused to aid those low-income families.

What was the result of this great Republican runaround? The real estate lobby won. And the people of the United States lost — lost homes they could have had, lost years of health and happiness in decent surroundings that might have been theirs.

I have gone into this story at length because it shows the way in which the Republican Party has thwarted the will of the people. Republican policies are depriving millions of families of the housing they need. Republican policies are keeping up prices of much of the food you eat and the clothing you buy.

And worst of all, these Republican policies, by permitting inflation to continue without proper curbs, are threatening the very foundations of our prosperity. They are not only injuring American living standards by high prices — they are also pushing the country into the terrible risk of another crash and another depression. That is why I must say to you that a Republican victory in November would be a victory for a policy that makes for hard times.

The Democratic Party is not perfect, but its leadership, its policies, and the great majority of the Democratic members of Congress stand squarely behind a policy aimed to preserve the prosperity of the people.

That, my friends, is the major issue in this campaign.

That is why I feel justified tonight in asking you to cast your votes, on election day, for a Democratic administration that has faith in the people and that plays fair with the people. And we shall need a Democratic Congress this time. We need a Democratic Congress to protect your pocketbooks, your home, your futures, and the happiness of your children.

Ever since I started out in this campaign, I have urged the people to exercise their rights in the government. The government is yours, if you are willing to accept the responsibility, and when you accept that responsibility, you will go to the polls on election day and vote your sentiments. I have been urging everybody in these United States to be sure to go to the polls on November 2 and to vote for themselves, vote for their own interests, vote for the people's interest. And when you do that, you can't do but one thing, and that is to vote the Democratic ticket straight.

A Democratic administration is what this country needs — what we all need. And it's very easy to get. All we have to do is to go to the polls and get it — if you do your duty. I am urging you with everything I have now — don't shirk your duty this time, as you did in 1946. You will get something worse than the 80th Congress, if you do!

NOTE: During his address the president referred to Senators Robert F. Wagner and Irving M. Ives of New York, Senator Allen J. Ellender of Louisiana, and Senator Robert A. Taft of Ohio.

OCTOBER 12

Address at the Springfield Armory
Springfield, Illinois (9 P.M.)

Senator Lucas and fellow Democrats of Illinois:

I wish I were half as good as Senator Lucas says I am. I might be able to fill the presidency as I know it ought to be filled, and as I pray that I may fill it.

I can't tell you how I appreciate the wonderful reception I have had in the great state of Illinois today. Every city where we have stopped has been just like this. It looks as if at every stop everybody for forty miles around was there — and I believe they were.

The cordiality of your greeting makes me believe that you are truly interested in the issues that are in this campaign — in my opinion, the most important campaign we will have for a generation.

I particularly want to pay tribute to the mayors of these various towns — the mayor of Decatur, the mayor of Danville, the mayor of Springfield. You have been exceedingly courteous and cordial to me and to my family, and we want to express our sincere thanks. And I want to say to you, if you ever come to Washington or if you will come to Missouri, we will try to give you the same kind of welcome.

You know, I am always glad to be in this great state, because it's a close neighbor of Missouri. I have a lot of friends in Illinois. I always had a lot of relatives too. I have found more relatives in Illinois and Kentucky and Missouri over the years that I think I can win an election if all my relatives vote for me.

Senator Barkley and I, you know, come from the same stock. The senator's ancestors stayed in Kentucky, and mine moved from Kentucky to Missouri, and those people in Kentucky who are not kinfolk of Senator Barkley's are kinfolk of mine.

We do understand the needs of that part of the United States that lies in the Mississippi Valley, but I think you will find that Senator Barkley and I also understand the needs of the nation as a whole and of the world. Each of us has had experience that is necessary to meet the conditions with which we are faced today. I hope you will weigh that carefully when you go to vote on the 2nd of November.

I'm glad to be here, too, to tell you how proud I am of the ticket the Democratic Party is offering to the voters of Illinois. Never within my memory has any party offered your state a finer team than Adlai Stevenson and Paul Douglas. I know that Adlai Stevenson is going to make a splendid governor. He is a fighter and comes of fighting stock. And when Senator Douglas gets down to Washington to work with your present great senator, Scott Lucas, it will be a good thing for Illinois and a good thing for the country as a whole, and for the world.

A man is known by the company he keeps, and I find myself in good company on your election ballot. Now, on the side, I want to say that I don't think I have celebrated or spent a more pleasant Columbus Day in the history of my life than I have today in Illinois. It has been a real celebration, one I think that has given the people some information that will do them good, and one I think that will do the country good. If old Columbus could come back and see what a great country he had discovered, my, how pleased he would be, I am sure!

I feel especially good about your election ballot, when I consider the unhappy situation of the Republican candidate for president in that respect. He certainly is lining up some queer characters. You ought to check the voting records of the candidates that he has been trying to get reelected to the United States Senate and the House of Representatives. Then you can judge for yourselves whether the elephant's got a "new look" and whether it means anything or not.

No one ever comes to this historic city without thinking of Abraham Lincoln. I just wonder tonight, as I have wondered many times in the past, what Lincoln would say if he could see how far the Republican Party has departed from the fundamental principles in which he so deeply believed. Lincoln came from the plain people, and he always believed in them. He put labor ahead of capital — he put people ahead of property — and principle above all else.

I just wonder what Lincoln would say if he could see how his party has become the tool of big business and special interests. How far do you suppose the real estate lobby would get with Abraham Lincoln? What do you suppose he would say to the power lobby and the railroad lobby? I have a notion that the only kind of lobby he would like would be a schoolteachers' lobby. The masters of the Republican Party today would have been the bitter enemies of Lincoln in his time, just as they are enemies of his principles today.

But I did not come here to talk about principles alone. I came to talk about putting principles to work for the good of the people.

Democrats are practical folks. We like to get down to cases and talk business. It's curious that our opponents, who claim to be so businesslike and so efficient, refuse to get down to specific issues. I don't blame them for trying to campaign on theory. They are afraid to tell the people where they stand on specific issues. The Republicans know they can't run on their record — that record is too bad. But you ought to know about their record. And since they won't tell you, I will.

I can't cover the whole story at one time, so tonight I will talk to you about the farm record of the Republicans. Here in Illinois you have a lot of farmers and a great many others who are dependent on farm prosperity. This story is of interest to everybody too, because it is a fair sample of the kind of treatment the people have been getting from the Republicans.

There are a few big questions every farmer — and every one of the rest of us — ought to ask himself before he decides how to vote on November 2. One of the questions each of us ought to ask is this: how well off was I in 1932, after the Republicans had been in office twelve years? How well off am I now, after having had Democratic presidents for the last sixteen years? For nearly all of us, the answer to that question is perfectly plain.

Some people would like you to think that the government had nothing to do with this — that the country just drifted into the depression without any help from the Republicans and drifted out into prosperity without any help from the Democrats. As a matter of fact, the government has a great deal to do with these things. The increasing prosperity we have enjoyed since 1933 has been due in a large part to government programs put into effect by the Democratic Party. The Republicans fought these programs for years, but lately they have come around, saying: "Me, too, but I can do it better."

Well, two-thirds of you stayed at home in 1946. That third that went to the polls elected the Republican 80th Congress, and you gave them a chance to show what they could do. And what did they do? Let's get back to the farm program.

The first thing they did was to cut the soil conservation program. They have been telling you how strong they were for soil conservation. I'll tell you how strong they were for it: the Republicans in the House of Representatives voted 12 to 1 to kill the agricultural conservation program entirely. That's how strong they were for it, although their platforms of 1940 and 1944, and even of 1948, said they were for soil conservation.

You ought to know this too: when they voted to kill that program, they automatically voted to kill the farmer-committee system. Those committees are made up of farmers and are elected by farmers to run the farm programs. As long as you have the farmer-committee system, you can laugh at the lies about bureaucrats coming out and running the farms. But if they kill the committees, one of two things will happen: either you won't have any farm program, or the bureaucrats will run whatever there is to run. There won't be much to run, I can tell you that. They will have to be Republican bureaucrats, too, because the Democrats will never allow that to happen, while we have the power to stop it.

The Republican attack on soil conservation and the committee system did not succeed in full. Democrats had voices, and we still had some votes in Congress. But remember this: the Republicans cut the agricultural conservation program exactly in half. Even for this election campaign they did not put back as much as they cut.

Let's look at some more of their performance. They tell you that they favor price supports. But while you sat out here on a powder keg waiting for prices to blow up, that Republican Congress lit a fuse.

They knew for a long time that price support legislation would expire at the end of this year. But for a year and a half after they took control of the Congress, they did absolutely nothing. The gentleman over there who said "nothing" to that question a while ago told the truth, if it ever was told. They did nothing for the people.

Then the first thing the Republicans did was to restrict the right of the

Commodity Credit Corporation to provide storage bins for grain. No longer can the government provide enough storage in rural areas to carry the surplus from the fat years until the lean years come. Farmers can't afford to go into the storage business to that extent. And the grain trade has been either unable or unwilling to do it.

This action by the Republicans will cost both farmers and consumers. It will benefit the speculative grain trade and the shipping interests. And that's all it will benefit. It will turn the farmers back to the speculators. If the farmers can't find storage facilities, they can't get support prices. And if you have to sell your corn for less than the support price for lack of storage, you will know that the blame lies squarely on the Republican Party and nowhere else.

While they were doing this to cripple price supports, the time was fast approaching when our major price support legislation would expire. Remember, they had had a year and a half to deal with this problem. But it was not until 5:00 on Sunday morning, in the last minutes of the congressional session, that they finally worked out a compromise price support bill. The Republicans were forced to pass something that would look good on the record for the election campaign. But at the very time they passed it, they were explaining that next year it could be amended or repealed. I had been begging them, ever since the Congress met, to meet that situation, but they couldn't do it until the last minute. They were afraid to go to the Republican convention in Philadelphia without doing some little thing, and that is what they did.

Just last month Republican senator Capper of Kansas, chairman of the Senate Committee on Agriculture in the 80th Congress, made a very significant statement in his weekly broadcast to Kansas. He openly predicted that there would be a drive in the next Congress to reduce the support price levels in 1949.

This uncertainty is unfair to all farmers, and especially unfair to those of you who are livestock producers, because you have to plan your operations a long time in advance. You need to know what you can count on, and on the basis of the record no farmer can count on the Republican attitude toward price supports. Only with a Democratic Congress and a Democratic president can you be sure that you will get a square deal on prices.

Some people want to know why I keep talking about the 80th Congress. Some of them seem to think that the Republican candidate for president has no connection with the record of the 80th Congress. I want to remind you of something. He is bound hand and foot by the record of the 80th Congress, and he is running on that record, and nothing else. In order to get the nomination, he endorsed the record of that Congress. That platform on which he is running gives it the warmest endorsement. He is trying to get the people to reelect every reactionary member of the 80th Congress, as you noticed when he came here to Illinois. Recently the Republican candidate stated that he was proud of the record of the 80th Congress.

Now, when I speak of the 80th Congress, I am speaking of the leadership of that Congress, the people who run it. I am not speaking of such men as Scott Lucas and other Democrats who served in that Congress. I am here to tell you that the leadership of that Congress — if you elect it this time — they will control it again, and we will have worse than an 80th Congress, if that is possible.

But we Democrats cannot be content merely to run against the Republican record, however black it may be. And although we are proud of the Democratic record, we are not content merely to run on our record.

We have a positive program for the future, and I want to be sure you know about it. This program has been spelled out in detail in messages I have sent to the Congress. Tonight I want to give you a brief and concrete statement of what the program is. But first, I want to remind you again of how much farmers and city people depend upon each other.

What I would like to tell you is very simple. I have said it again and again in this campaign. If you are a farmer, your customers are in the cities, and most of them are men and women who work for a living. Unless they get good wages, they can't pay good farm prices. And as for labor, the best market for the products of industry is the farmer. Unless the farmer gets a fair price — a parity price — for his crops, he can't buy the clothes and the tools and the automobiles and the radios and the other things which labor helps to manufacture.

When the farmer votes for a Republican Party that proposes to smash the strength of labor, the farmer is not voting just for a cut in the wages of the city workers. He is voting to cut his own income. He is voting to reduce his own prices. He is voting to have the Republican Party do a repeat performance of the agricultural depression of the 1920s.

This is now the most prosperous nation the world ever saw. And we can keep it that way. I propose to tell you how we can keep it that way, particularly as to how agriculture is concerned. There is only one sane national policy for agriculture, and that is a policy of organized, sustained, and realistic abundance. We must not only produce abundantly, but we must market, distribute, and consume the abundance we produce.

Our farmers are producing far more than before the war, and, with continuing prosperity, they can produce even more. The people are eating more and better food and generally living better. Many people, however, are not yet able to supply their needs. When all our people can get as much as they should have, then we will have no danger of farm surpluses.

In order for our people to get all they need, we must maintain high levels of employment. If unemployment should occur, we must be ready immediately to take up the slack. We must also maintain good export outlets.

Now, this is what I believe in. Here are the main outlines of the agricultural program we must have:

1. We must have on a permanent basis a system of flexible price supports for agricultural commodities. Price supports and related measures help us keep our farm production adjusted to shifting market requirements. They are also required by the very nature of our economy. Farm prices are unstable in relation to other prices. And farm price trouble can lead to depression, which cuts the markets and further depresses agriculture. Parity must be our continuing goal.

2. We must expand our soil conservation program and put a stop to the waste of our agricultural resources. By using our land wisely, we can produce abundantly and permanently. But wasteful use of the soil is national suicide.

3. We must continue and strengthen our programs to assure adequate consumption of agricultural products. In this I include scientific research, efforts to encourage world trade through agreements and other means, the school lunch program, and further efforts to improve the diets of low-income families. We must never again allow our people to go hungry while surpluses are going to waste.

4. We must continue to develop means of meeting special agricultural problems. For example, we must protect the right of farmers to do business through cooperatives. We must extend rural electrification. We must have better housing, better roads, and better educational facilities for our farmers.

The policy and the programs I have mentioned are essential to the future welfare of agriculture. They are essential to the welfare and prosperity of this whole nation and of the world. A policy of democratic abundance is the best answer in the world to the threat of communism. It is a policy that contributes toward world peace.

Thanks to the Democratic administrations of the past, we have much of the legislation we need to follow a policy of organized, sustained, and realistic abundance. I asked that 80th Congress to add the missing pieces and to provide adequate support for the programs we have. The Republican leadership refused.

I wish that Wall Street crowd would let their candidate stamp his "me, too" on the agricultural policy that my party and my administration stand for. I wish we had a least as much bipartisan support for our agricultural policy as we have for our foreign policy. But unfortunately agricultural policy is very much a partisan matter at this time.

The enemies of the farmer feel pretty cocky. They tell us the farmer is fat and happy and not worried about anything. They picture the farmer in a private airplane or a fine new car, and they laugh and say the farmer won't pay any attention to Truman.

They say the same thing about labor. Labor has been put in its place, they say, and is going to get more of the same.

I wish they were right in saying you don't have a thing to worry about. You are more prosperous than you ever were under the Republicans. But I want you to be as prosperous as the people who are saying you are already too prosperous.

As a Democrat, I believe in prosperity for the many, and not for just a few. I believe that the farmer and the industrial worker, and the miner and the businessman, will prosper together or they will fail together. I reject the reactionary idea that there are second-class citizens who were meant to be nothing but hewers of wood and drawers of water. I maintain that every man, woman, and child in the United States is entitled to a decent living and to equal justice in a free land.

To that end, we of the Democratic Party pledge our strength and our courage. We shall never rest until, by God's grace, we have attained that goal.

NOTE: The opening words "Senator Lucas" referred to Senator Scott W. Lucas of Illinois. Later he referred to Mayor James A. Hedrick of Decatur, Mayor G. N. Hicks of Danville, Mayor Harry Eielson of Springfield, Democratic candidate for senator Paul H. Douglas, and Democratic candidate for governor Adlai E. Stevenson, all of Illinois; and Senator Arthur Capper of Kansas. The address was carried on a nationwide radio broadcast.

★ ★ ★ ★ ★ ★ ★ ★ ★ ★ ★ ★ ★ ★ ★ ★ ★ ★

OCTOBER 14

Rear Platform Remarks
Winona, Minnesota (11:45 A.M.)

Thank you — thank you very much. I can't tell you how very much I appreciate the cordial welcome which has been extended to me by the citizens of Minnesota. It is evident that the citizens of Minnesota are interested in the welfare of this great nation and that they want to know what the issues are in this campaign. And believe me, I have been telling them what the issues are!

I have been traveling through Minnesota since yesterday at noon, when I crossed the St. Louis River and arrived in Duluth. It has been a thrilling experience. It has not only been fine to see your rich farmland, and the great grain elevators, and your cities enjoying greater prosperity than ever before in history, but it has been especially rewarding to travel through Minnesota and meet you fellow Minnesotans and your great candidate for the Senate, Mayor Hubert Humphrey, and your fine candidates for Congress, and Karl Rolvaag, whom I am sure you are going to send to the Congress. You are also going to send Mayor Humphrey of Minneapolis to the Senate, and then we will have people in the 81st Congress with whom the president can work.

The crowds that have come down to the stations prove beyond any doubt that you people are determined to elect a liberal, Democratic president and a liberal, Democratic congressional delegation when you go to the polls on November 2.

You know that this prosperity that I have seen all through Minnesota did not just happen. It was brought about by sixteen years of control of the government by Democratic administrations. Back in the Republican depression year of 1932, Minnesota farmers made less than a quarter of a billion dollars. Last year, the income of Minnesota's farmers was a billion and half dollars. That is the difference between the right side of a proposition so that everybody gets his fair share of the national income, and that approach which gives only the special privileged few the national income.

One key in the Democratic prosperity program was the Commodity Credit Corporation. One job of the Commodity Credit Corporation was to increase grain storage facilities so that bumper crops could be marketed over a longer period of time, thus making it unnecessary for the farmer to sell all his wheat or his corn to big speculators at very cheap prices.

The Commodity Credit Corporation did a wonderful job for years, and then something happened to it. Two-thirds of you stayed at home from the polls in 1946, and the Republicans got control of the Congress. That 80th "do-nothing" Congress came about because you didn't do your duty as voters.

The farmers are just now beginning to realize what that means to them. Big business is against any aid to the farmers, and the Republican leaders in Congress are the errand boys of big business and special privilege.

That is why the Republican 80th "do-nothing" Congress — I mean "do nothing" for the people; they did something for the special interests all right — that is why that Congress cut the Commodity Credit Corporation grain storage program down to almost nothing. Now there is a bumper crop, and the Commodity Credit Corporation no longer has the authority to provide storage space, and the farmers are being forced to sell their grain to speculators way below support prices. And that situation will get worse. It has just now started. Right now, speculators are buying corn below the support price. That is just plain robbery of the farmers, and the farmers owe that to the 80th Congress. Now, if you send an 81st Congress back like that one, you will get treated worse than that.

This Republican sabotage of the Commodity Credit Corporation has not only hurt the farmer. It has also hurt every industry and every business in the state of Minnesota, because as you all know, your prosperity depends upon farm prosperity.

It is up to you whether or not this Republican special-interest domination of Congress is going to continue. If you don't vote on November 2, the chances are that the special interests will proceed to control the country and the Congress and the government.

Now, two-thirds of you didn't vote in 1946 — and look what you got! Don't do that again. Go out and do your duty on election day. This election will decide the future of the Commodity Credit Corporation and the farm program. It will decide much more than that for the whole country. It will decide whether soil conservation and reforestation go forward with the Democrats or go backwards with the Republicans. It will decide whether we will be able to bring down the cost of living with the Democrats or keep on with sky-rocketing prices under a Republican program.

It will decide whether we have slum clearance and low-rent housing and good rural housing with the Democrats or whether we shall have a housing shortage under a Republican administration. It will decide whether we will have full development of our great river system, so that cities like Winona can develop into great river ports, or whether eastern power and railroad lobbies get control under the Republicans and stop the development of our great waterways.

Every one of these issues is at stake in this election. When you realize how much this election means to you and to your own prosperity, I am confident you will turn out on election day and vote for your own interest. You are voting for yourselves. When you vote for yourselves, you will vote for the interests of all the people, and that is you and me and everybody else.

When you do that, you can't help but send a Democratic Congress back to Washington, and you can't help but have a Democratic president in the White House. And then your president won't be troubled with the housing shortage; he will have a house to live in for the next four years.

This is one of the most important elections this country has faced in forty years, and it will have its effects for generations to come. So be sure and do your duty on that election day. Go out and vote, and I am here to tell you that if everybody in this country expresses his opinion and votes, I am not worried about the results.

★ ★ ★ ★ ★ ★ ★ ★ ★ ★ ★ ★ ★ ★ ★ ★

OCTOBER 14

Address at the University of Wisconsin

Madison (4:25 P.M.)

Mr. Chairman and fellow Democrats of Wisconsin:

I am more than happy to have this opportunity to talk to the people of Wisconsin. My secretary of the interior, Julius Krug, is a native of this great city, and he is a magnificent public official.

I am especially glad to be in Madison, which I remember was named by a national magazine as the perfect city to live in. Wisconsin is a state which gave us "Fighting Bob" LaFollette; a state which has led all others in sound, progressive legislation; a state which has served as the model and the inspiration for all the other states in the country in the way in which its university has worked with the leaders of the state in pioneering a better way of life for all the people.

Wisconsin needs to regain her position in leadership in the cause of liberalism in the United States. Wisconsin about-faced a short time ago, and they ought to come back and get in step with the people who are going forward. You can do that by rallying all your liberal forces behind the common banner — the banner of the Democratic Party.

I am pleased that the followers of old Fighting Bob have recognized that the Democratic Party is the party which has their interests at heart. I am very pleased that a leader of the old Progressive Party of Wisconsin, Carl Thompson, is the Democratic candidate for governor in this election. And I think you will do yourselves a favor, in this congressional district, if you send Horace Wilkie to the Congress. These men have joined the Democratic ranks because they know it is the only truly liberal party today.

What happened to the Republican Party in Wisconsin has been repeated on a national level. The 80th Congress was the tragic answer to all those who hoped that the elephant had acquired a "new look." That 80th Congress was controlled — a controlled Congress, where lobbyists pulled the strings and the people got stung.

An excellent example of how we got legislation by lobby, instead of laws to meet our needs, is found in the story of the Taft-Ellender-Wagner Housing Bill. I would like to tell you a little about that bill.

It was sponsored by two Democrats and one Republican. It had been developed through three years of study. During this time, hundreds of thousands of words of testimony from every corner of the United States was collected. This study showed that the United States, the most powerful nation on earth, had failed to provide decent housing for its citizens. Three million American families are living doubled up with other families. Five million families are living in housing that isn't fit for an American citizen to live in. Five million are living in slums that are rotting out the cores of our great cities. We are falling further behind every year as construction fails to keep up with our needs.

There is nothing more un-American than a city slum. Slums are the breeding spots of crime, sickness, and chaos in every large city in America.

Our farm housing is something that Americans don't like to talk about either. More than half our farm homes do not meet modern American standards.

The Democratic Party has placed at the top of its program an answer to the housing problem. But what do the Republicans say? They say that private builders can do the job. They say this in spite of the fact that private builders are not doing the job.

This year the real estate is crowing that more homes are being built than were built in the former peak year of 1926. I ask you, what kind of hope is there when we brag about passing a mark set twenty-two years ago, when the needs, the job, and the problems were very much smaller?

But the real estate lobby killed the Americans' hopes for a federal housing law to help meet our needs. Its instrument was the leadership of the Republican Party. When the lobby-controlled Republican chairman of the Banking and Currency Committee stated at the end of the second session of the 80th Congress that he would not even allow the House of Representatives to vote on the bill, every single Democratic member of that committee turned against him and voted for the bill.

There is a powerful committee in the House of Representatives called the Rules Committee. That committee decides what bills the House may be allowed to consider. In the second session of the 80th Congress, every Democrat in the Rules Committee voted to let the House of Representatives act on the housing bill. Every Republican on the Rules Committee voted against allowing the House to consider it. That is typical of the difference between the Democratic and the Republican attitudes towards the housing bill that we so badly need.

In the Senate, 70 percent of the Democrats voted for that housing bill; 70 percent of the Republicans in the Senate voted against the bill and for a substitute phony housing bill sponsored by this same real estate lobby. They kept the housing bill from passing.

That is what happened to housing legislation in the 80th Congress. That is why we do not now have a federal program for slum clearance, low-rent public housing, and low-rent rural housing. I have been told that the real estate lobby is bragging that they licked the president of the United States. Well, let me tell you something — I'm not licked yet by any means.

I think I know what the American people want, and I promise you that I am trying to see that they get it. I know that every veterans organization, the American Conference of Mayors, farm groups, women's groups, church groups, and most of the American citizens endorse that housing bill that I tried to put through last session, and I am going to carry this message to every town and village in America.

If you want housing, you had better vote the Democratic ticket. I remember about twenty years ago that a popular Republican slogan was, "Two cars in every garage." This year their slogan is, "Two families in every garage."

I wish I had time to tell you all about the other ways that 80th Congress failed the American people, how they failed to enact a health bill or provide federal aid for states to meet their acute problems in education, how they knocked the props out from under farm prosperity, and how they so greatly weakened the strength of organized labor. When you learn the truth about all those issues, you will be as amazed as I was when the Republican candidate for president said that he was proud of the record of that 80th Congress. I just don't know what he is proud of.

You people in Wisconsin are fortunate in having real progressives running for office this year on the Democratic ticket. You have men like Horace Wilkie, a World War II veteran who has studied the housing problem carefully and was one of the leaders of the National Veterans Conference. Horace Wilkie can truly represent the liberals of Madison, and of course, you have men like Carl Thompson, who will make one of the best governors Wisconsin ever had.

These men believe, as I do and as the whole Democratic Party does, that we must have firm and fair laws to bring down the cost of living, that we must have a housing bill and a national health program, that we must ensure a fair deal to farmers, to labor, to the small businessman, and to the white-collar worker. They believe, as I believe, in government for the benefit of all the people, not in government for the benefit of special privileges.

Now, we are faced with a real problem — your problem. For the first time in history you are going to have a chance to decide whether you want a government run by the people or whether you want a government run by special interests. This country in 1947 had the greatest national income in the history of the world — $217 billion. That income was reasonably fairly distributed, between the farmer and laboring man and the businessman — particularly the small businessman.

Now the acts, and the effects of the acts, of this 80th Congress are trying to upset that balanced program. They want special privilege, because the first thing they did was to pass the rich man's tax bill, and now they are soliciting all those rich men for campaign funds to put out a propaganda campaign against me and my administration.

That income tax bill would let a fellow who made $60 a week save about

$1.50 a week — or $1.60 maybe — but a fellow who got $100,000 a year saves $16,000, and they are inviting him to turn half of that over to the Republican campaign committee. A lot of them will do it, too.

Now, you people can vote for your own best interests by voting for yourselves on election day, or you can vote for this crowd that has made the policy of the Republican Party in the 80th Congress. I don't believe you are going to do that. I think you are going to go to the polls and vote for the American way of life.

NOTE: The opening words "Mr. Chairman" referred to Carl Thompson, Democratic candidate for governor of Wisconsin. The president later referred to Robert M. LaFollette, former senator from Wisconsin, and Horace W. Wilkie, Democratic candidate for Congress from Wisconsin's Second District.

OCTOBER 18

Address at the American Legion Convention

Dinner Key, Miami, Florida (2 P.M.)

Mr. Commander, members of the auxiliary, ladies and gentlemen:

This is an opportunity I have been looking forward to for thirty years, and I finally made it. I have chosen this occasion to discuss with you some very important matters, and I am glad to be here today as a delegate from Missouri first, as a comrade-in-arms, and as commander in chief of the armed forces of the United States.

Legionnaires have been meeting together for a long time. This makes the thirtieth year that the legion has met to keep strong the ties that bind men together, who fought side by side for their country. In those years the legion has been serving our country in peace as well as in war. And nobody knows that better than I do. I am happy to see the younger men of World War II joining and strengthening our organization, which has never failed to be vigilant for the welfare and security of this great country of ours.

I have looked forward to this opportunity of counseling with you as veterans. Among our countrymen, you understand best of all the tragic meaning of war. You learned the hard way how to hate it. Today I want to share with you my views about the things that lie nearest to our hearts — peace and freedom in the world.

As president of the United States, it has been my duty to find men to staff our efforts for security and peace. It's an altogether different task to secure good men after the shooting stops than it is to secure them while the fighting is going on.

It has been my duty to initiate and approve the great proposals which have advanced both for our society and the recovery of the free nations of the world. As your chief executive, I know of the patriotic efforts of men of both parties to support those policies.

The plain fact remains, however, that while the president of the United States can delegate authority, he has the responsibility, under the Constitution of the United States, for the conduct of our foreign affairs. In that capacity, I want to stress something which I am sure every veteran and every real American will approve. So long as I am president, the United States will not carry a chip on its shoulder. As I have said time and again, that I would rather see a lasting peace in the world than to be president of the United States.

In recent months, the trend of events has caused us deep concern. The great need today is for action to strengthen the United Nations in dealing with the disputes which now challenge its authority — action to create an improved atmosphere for all future negotiations looking toward peace.

Lately, in Europe and even here in the United States, there has been loose and irresponsible talk to the effect that the United States is deliberately following a course that leads to war. That is a plain and deliberate lie.

We have taken, and we will continue to take, a firm position where our rights are threatened. But our firmness should not be mistaken for a warlike spirit. The world has learned that it is weakness and appeasement that invite aggression. A firm position on reasonable grounds offers the best hope of peace, and we have been open to reason at every point.

We recognize the principle of mutual conciliation as a basis for peaceful negotiation, but this is very different from appeasement. While we will always strive for peace, this country will never consent to any compromise of the principles of freedom and human rights. We will never be a party to the kind of compromise which the world sums up in the disgraced name of Munich.

Our purpose, from the end of the war to the present, has never changed.

It has been to create a political and economic framework in which a lasting peace may be constructed.

Let me remind you how we have sought to carry out that purpose. In the past two years, the United States has made three major moves of foreign policy in the European area. Each move has been tied in with the work of the United Nations. Each move has been designated to reduce the dangers of chaos and war.

The first move was made in March 1947, when we offered economic and military aid to Greece and Turkey, then threatened by Communist aggression. Three months later, we began our second major move — the great program for European economic recovery. With American help under this plan, sixteen European nations are making a joint effort, unprecedented in history, to overcome heavy economic losses suffered in the great war. A number of these countries have already increased their production and improved their financial stability. It is not too much to say that this plan holds the key for the economic future of Europe and the world.

Our third major move was the joint action of the United States, Great Britain, and France in establishing a working, but by no means final, economic organization for the western zones of Germany, under allied military control. This step was undertaken to encourage the economic revival of Germany, under proper safeguards, so as to aid the recovery of all Western Europe and promote stability. We have also been giving support and encouragement to the organization of the Western European Union.

These moves in the field of foreign policy have had as their goal the peace of the world. Naturally, this country was at the same time protecting its own interests. No nation can afford to disregard self-interest.

I think it is fair to say that American policy has revealed an unusual degree of enlightenment. We have taken it as a first principle that our interest is bound up with the peace and economic recovery of the rest of the world. Accordingly, we have worked for all three together — world peace, world economic recovery, and the welfare of our own nation.

It is plain that world peace and economic recovery cannot be achieved in an atmosphere of political disorder and revolution. We have therefore felt it essential to help stabilize nations which welcomed our aid and whose democratic traditions or aspirations invited our friendship. At the same time, we can maintain our own economic stability and keep up a military establishment commensurate with our leadership for peace.

As president, I have inaugurated economic and military operations which will enable this great nation to meet its obligations. This policy must be carried to success.

Our policy is not now and never has been directed against the Soviet Union. On the contrary, we recognize that the peace of the world depends on increasing understanding and a better working relationship between the Soviet Union and the democratic nations.

The problem which now confronts this country and the world reduces itself to one basic question: can we so reconcile the interests of the Western powers and the interests of the Soviet Union as to bring about an enduring peace?

Let me say here again, and as plainly as I can, that the government of this country, like the American people as a whole, detests the thought of war. We are shocked by its brutality and sickened by its waste of life and wealth. And we know from experience that war creates many more problems than it solves. We know that all the world, and especially the continent of Europe, has nothing to gain from war and everything to lose.

The horrors that modern war inflicts on innocent people are known to all Americans. The use of atomic weapons and bacteriological warfare, in particular, might unleash new forces of destruction which would spare no nation. All of us are well acquainted with that fact. We know, too, that if war should come upon us again, the loss in life, the strain on our physical resources and even on our democratic institutions, might be greater than we care to contemplate.

The government of the United States rejects the concept of war as a means of solving international differences.

However, I think we are realistic about the alternative to war. In international politics, new and serious difficulties are continually arising. It will be a long while before the great powers constitute the friendly family of nations which is so often described as "one world."

Our need is to work out with cool detachment a practical adjustment of our troubles with other nations as they may arise. That is the attitude in which we have been trying to find reasonable solutions to the critical problems which now confront us.

Unfortunately — and I say that advisedly — unfortunately, a dark fog of distrust has risen between the Soviet Union and the West, distorting and confusing our relations. It is clear that little progress is likely to be made in settling disputes between the Western powers and Soviet Russia, so long as there is so much distrust. If that distrust is to be dispelled, there needs to be evidence of long-range peaceful purposes — evidence that will enable the world to shake off the fear of war, reduce the burden of armaments, and concentrate on useful economic activities.

In recently considering sending a special emissary to Moscow, my purpose was to ask Premier Stalin's cooperation in dispelling the present poisonous atmosphere of distrust which now surrounds the negotiations between the Western powers and the Soviet Union. My emissary was to convey the seriousness and sincerity of the people of the United States in their desire for peace.

This proposal had no relation to existing negotiations within the scope of the United Nations or the Council of Foreign Ministers. Far from cutting across these negotiations, the purpose of this mission was to improve the atmosphere in which they must take place and so help in producing fruitful and peaceful results.

At this time I want to make it perfectly clear that I have not departed one step from my determination to utilize every opportunity to work for peace. Whenever an appropriate opportunity arises, I shall act to further the interests of peace within the framework of our relations with our allies and the work of the United Nations. I am working for peace, and I shall continue to work for peace.

Both we and the Soviet Union have a fundamental job to do — the job of raising the living standards of our peoples.

We must remember that many a serious crisis has in the past been resolved without war. We must remember that the struggle for existence among nations, as among individual men, goes on all the time and expresses itself in many ways other than war. We must remember that rivalry among nations is an old story. History shows that rival powers can exist peacefully in the world.

Patience must be our watchword. When the destiny of all mankind is at stake, we need to exercise all the patience we can muster. We should utilize every opportunity to strengthen the United Nations for the great undertakings which lie ahead.

The people of the world are looking to their leaders to dispel the fog of distrust which now confuses the approach to peace. At the present moment, I would only add that our nation has never failed to meet the great crises of its history with honor and devotion to its ideals. My friends, and fellow Legionnaires, we shall spare no effort to achieve the peace on which the entire destiny of the human race depends.

NOTE: The president's opening words "Mr. Commander" referred to James F. O'Neil, national commander of the American Legion. The thirtieth annual convention was attended by eight thousand legionnaires.

★ ★ ★ ★ ★ ★ ★ ★ ★ ★ ★ ★ ★ ★ ★ ★ ★

OCTOBER 19

Address at the State Fairgrounds
Raleigh, North Carolina (3:05 P.M.)

Governor Cherry, distinguished guests, and fellow Democrats of North Carolina:

I can't tell you how very much I appreciate the most cordial welcome I have received in the capital city of this great state today. Your governor has been exceedingly kind and cordial to me and to my family, and we have spent a most pleasant morning. The governor took us to the Governor's Mansion for luncheon, and I want to say to you that it was *some* luncheon. Outside of Missouri, I never saw another one like it.

I am happy to be on this platform today with all these good North Carolina Democrats who are serving the nation. To hear the chairman call the roll, it sounded as if North Carolina is running the nation. If they had the presidency, they would be. I have had some very fine friends from North Carolina, and I would like to name all of them, if I could, but it would take the rest of the afternoon, and I wouldn't have a chance to make my speech schedule.

There is one in particular I would like to mention, however, and one I made under secretary of the treasury, and I also appointed him to be ambassador to Great Britain. He was a former governor of North Carolina — Max Gardner — a wonderful man.

And I want to say to your next governor, Kerr Scott, that I appreciate most highly what he had to say when he was here before this microphone, and I know that the next senator, and the next junior senator from North Carolina — another friend of mine, Mel Broughton — will represent North Carolina, as North Carolina has always been represented in the United States, honorably and efficiently.

As I said before, if I took the time to mention and compliment the able and efficient public servants from North Carolina who are now serving the government in Washington, I wouldn't have time to do anything else this afternoon.

For a long time now, some of my North Carolina friends have been telling me I ought to take a look at this great state fair of yours. It wasn't necessary to urge me very much. I have always liked to go to fairs. But I do have one complaint. Now they make me one of the exhibits, and I don't get a chance to look at the others very much.

It's a wonderful thing to be the president of the United States, the greatest honor that can come to any man in the world. But I have lived in Independence, Missouri, since I was six years old, and for fifty-eight years nobody paid much attention to me in Independence, except to be friendly with me and say "Hello, Harry" when I went there. Now when I go to my old home in Independence, it takes the whole Independence police force and half the Secret Service to get me in the front door. I don't know what happens to people.

I can remember back the first time I ever saw a president, and that was in 1904, and I ran three blocks to get to take a look at the then candidate for president, and he was running on the Republican ticket too. So I know that it's the office they want to see and not the man. I have to remember that all the time. If you don't, you get a bad case of "Potomac fever" in Washington.

This fall I have visited several state fairs. I met thousands of prosperous farm folk there, and it made me proud of the grand old Democratic Party to see so many farmers who had been rescued from Republican depression and given the break they deserved. You know, the farmers never were as prosperous in this country as they are now — the first time in the history of the country that the farmers have received a fair share of the national income.

Not long ago I had to roll into the fair at Oklahoma City at a speed of fifty miles an hour. That was because I stopped to talk to so many people along the way that my train was a little late. But the train crew, being good Democrats, saw to it that I got there. I'm surprised the Republican candidate didn't order them shot at sunrise.

Out in Dexter, Iowa, I met a great farm gathering for the National Plowing Contest. And we plowed under a lot of Republicans out there.

I want to say that I used to run a plow back on the farm thirty years ago, and I told them that I would like to try my hand at it, if they could get me a team of four mules, but they ran everything with a tractor. So I told them I didn't want to be like the Republicans, I didn't want to turn the clock back, so if they wanted to go ahead and run it with a tractor, it was all right with me.

I also got a chance to look over some of the fine new farm machines they were exhibiting. And I want to report to you that, among all the exhibits I have seen, there has been a great omission. Nowhere in the United States this year have I seen a single exhibit of that famous North Carolina farm invention — that product of ingenuity and hard times, of personal despair and political mockery, the Hoover cart.

You remember the Hoover cart — I didn't find that in Iowa, or anywhere else — the remains of the old tin lizzie being pulled by a mule because you couldn't afford to buy a new car, you couldn't afford to buy gas for the old one.

You remember. First you had the Hoovercrats, and then you had the Hoover carts. One always follows the other. Bear that in mind now, carefully.

By the way, I asked the Department of Agriculture at Washington about this Hoover cart. They said it is the only automobile in the world that eats oats. They don't recommend it, and neither do I.

I don't mind being an exhibit here myself. I think I belong right here. I'm a homegrown American farm product. That product is just about the same in Missouri as it is in North Carolina.

And I'm proud of the breed I represent — the completely unterrified form of American democracy. I stand for the simple, straightforward, straight-line Democratic Party. That party has always stood for government in the interest of the farmer and the workingman and for all the people of this great country. That party does not represent special privilege; it represents the whole people.

And anytime you have any doubts about the Democratic Party, all you need to do is take a good look at the Republican Party. That will always bring you right back where you belong.

This year we've all had a good look at the Republican Party and their candidate, and it's made me fighting mad. That's why I'm here today talking to you good people of North Carolina.

This year the Republicans are putting on a terrific advertising campaign in order to sell you the same old brand of Hoover carts. They're spending money in carload lots and are buying themselves all kinds of strange bedfellows. But there are some things that are not for sale in this country.

I don't believe that they're going to get away with it. Everybody — North and South — knows there's only one choice in this campaign. Either the standard Republicans will buy the election or the standard Democrats will win it. Other parties simply don't stand a chance.

For a southerner that ought not to be a hard choice. You know what Republicanism means in North Carolina and everywhere else in the South. First, it means the rule of the carpetbaggers. Then it means rule by moneybaggers. Either way, it means a rule that treats the South and the West as colonies to be exploited commercially and held down politically.

Republicanism means that the federal government is controlled by the powerful men and the greedy Wall Street interests that want cheap labor and the cheap farm products. Republicanism puts the almighty dollar first and is not above using a little tidelands oil money to grease the way to power.

Today big-money Republicanism is on the march, and to beat it we've all got to stand together. That's where we Democrats belong — together — shoulder to shoulder.

We are the great middle-of-the-road party — the party of the farmers and the workers and the small businessmen and the party of the young people. We all belong together. I believe in loyalty as the great force in politics — the loyalty of free men and women, freely given and honorably received. But above all I treasure the basic principle of democracy itself — the right to disagree among ourselves, without letting differences of opinion lead us into temptation or to betray our own best interests.

That is why I do not worry too much about the many violent arguments we Democrats have. I think that there will be plenty of Democrats on election day, as long as we retain respect for free speech and get a fair and honest count at the polls. Just the same, I hope that somewhere in North Carolina you have a Hoover cart on display — lest you forget that the Republicans want you to take another ride in that same old wagon.

In the 1920s the Republican Party could not fight the depression. It was incapable of bold action for the people. Big business owners of that dismal party said there was nothing to do but "ride it out." Ride it out! You did — in Hoover carts.

Today the Republican Party stands convicted of being incapable of fighting inflation. Some of its present leaders have tried to put the blame for inflation on farm prices. They want you to ride it out — ride it out! — in Hoover carts. It was under a Democratic administration that Hoover carts gave way to real automobiles with plenty of gasoline in them.

Here at a great agricultural fair, let's take a look at your agricultural record in North Carolina in the Democratic years behind us. Your old-time money crops are doing all right. Last year your tobacco brought you $380 million. In the Hoover year of 1932, your tobacco brought you $43 million. The price of tobacco got down to 8½ cents in the Republican depression. This year it is running close to 50 cents.

You don't depend on cotton as much as you used to. But you're getting more than three times as much money for your cotton as you got in either the Republican depression of 1932 or the Republican "boom" year of 1929.

Your cash receipts are running eight times what they were in 1932. You didn't make that trip in a Hoover cart.

This year your milk and eggs alone are worth almost as much as your total farm production was worth in 1932. Think of that! Milk and eggs in North Carolina worth as much as your farm production was in 1932!

What I say of North Carolina is true of the whole advancing South in the years since the Democrats came to office in Washington under Franklin Roosevelt. It was the Democratic Party that rescued agriculture in North Carolina, in the South, in the whole United States.

The Democratic farm program treated credit as a farmer's tool instead of a rich man's toy. We made credit available to farmers on fair terms for the first time in American history.

The Democratic party inaugurated the nationwide soil program.

The Democratic farm program brought you rural electrification. Back in 1935, only about three farms out of a hundred in North Carolina had electric service. Today the figure is about seventy in every hundred. And when the REA loans that are already approved are turned into actual power lines, eighty out of every hundred North Carolina farms will have electricity.

The Democratic farm program brought you farm crop insurance. The Democratic farm program expanded and intensified scientific research. The Democratic Party brought you support prices.

The Democratic farm program and the hard work of American farm families rescued agriculture from its sickness and made it strong again. Because of this, our agriculture was a source of strength to the nation when we had to fight a war. When our lives and our freedom depended on it, our agriculture was equal to the task.

Thanks to the Democratic Party, this is your story — the story of progress from the depths of despair to the heights of strength. You have a highly productive, efficient, and profitable agriculture, because you used the Democratic farm program and your own hard work to make it so.

But today the wreckers are at work. The Republican Party for years fought the Democratic Party farm program. When they saw it couldn't be changed, then they changed tactics. Republican spokesmen are now saying: "Me, too — only we can do it better." What they mean is, they can do you better!

Two years ago the nation gave the Republicans their chance in Congress. The Republicans immediately slashed the soil conservation program. In fact, the Republicans in the House of Representatives voted to keep out the agricultural conservation program altogether. That was also a vote to kill the farmer-committee system that operates your program of price supports and tobacco quotas. We beat this outrageous attack on self-rule in farming, but the Republicans did cut the agricultural conservation program in half.

They cut the rural electrification program. They undermined the Commodity Credit Corporation. They killed the International Wheat Agreement. They crippled the reciprocal trade agreements program on which the foreign markets for your tobacco and cotton depend.

They subjected farm cooperatives to a fear campaign under threat of a death tax. They cut the budget for the new research and marketing activities. They tried to kill the farm tenant purchase program.

And, now, despite the belated protestation of the Republican candidate, they are showing that they want to alter and destroy the whole structure of price supports for farm products. Even the Republican chairman of the Senate Committee on Agriculture has warned that an effort is being made to make the farmer the "goat" for high prices in the United States.

This attack on the price support system comes at a time when many farm prices are dropping and the price support program is of the greatest importance to the farmer and to the United States. The Democratic Party originated the farm price support program. We built it out of hard experience. We built it for the benefit of the entire nation — not only the farmer but the consumer as well.

The purpose of price supports is to prevent farm prices from falling to ruinously low levels. But the Republicans don't tell the city consumers that these supports apply only when farm prices have dropped below parity. They don't tell the people in the cities that everybody is really better off when the farmer gets decent prices.

The support price for wheat is not responsible for the price of bread. When wheat prices were going up, the price of bread rose steadily. It went up from 10 cents a loaf to 11 cents to 12 cents to 13 cents to 14 cents. Now wheat prices have fallen a dollar a bushel. But the price of bread has not come down one single cent. The same with cotton. Nobody can blame the cost of a shirt on the cotton that goes into it. The cost of tobacco in a cigarette is very, very small — a fraction of a cent.

The truth of the matter is that by encouraging the record production of the last few years, the support program has actually kept consumer prices down. Those who are willfully trying to discredit the price support system do not want farmers to be prosperous. They believe in low prices for farmers, cheap wages for labor, and high profits for big corporations. That is what they call "efficiency."

You cannot dodge the issue. You stand for the Democratic farm program, or you stand for the Republican wrecking crew of the 80th Congress. You stand with the Democratic Party, or you stand against it. You stand for the Democratic Party, or for all practical purposes you stand with the Republican Party. You stand for continuing progress of all the people, or you stand with those who for so many years thought farmers and southerners should be content in a colonial status and on a second-class economic level.

I know that you good people of North Carolina are not responsible for the Republicans in the 80th Congress. But we can all learn a lesson from them. They have given us a sharp warning of what the Republican Party stands for today. And their record shows that the Republican Party stands for the same thing today that it did under Herbert Hoover.

That is the record on which the Republican presidential candidate wants to be elected — that is the one on which he wants to be unified. He has endorsed the record of the 80th Congress, which began the scuttling of the Democratic farm program. He is running on a platform that endorses the record of the 80th Congress. He is going around the country asking people to reelect the worst members of the 80th Congress. He says he is proud of that 80th Congress. Well, if anybody with the welfare of this country at heart can be proud of that Congress, there is something wrong with his mind or his heart.

And when I say "Congress," I mean the leaders of that Congress. There are a lot of good men in that Congress, but they have nothing to say about the policy, because they are in the minority. I want you to make those men members of the majority.

The Republicans ask you to vote for them, but they don't care whether you vote for the Republican candidate or for a third-, fourth-, or fifth-party candidate. They know that a vote for any third- or fourth- or fifth-party candidate is the same as a vote for the Republican candidate. They hope they can fool enough of the people this time to capture the election by wasted Democratic votes.

I don't think you want to take another chance on the Hoover brand of Republicanism. I don't think you have to be hit on the head twice to know who hit you the first time. I don't think you are going to be the victims this time of the old Republican doctrine: "If you can't convince them, confuse them."

I think you know who your real friends are and who your enemies are. I feel pretty sure that in 1948 the South is not hankering for another ride in a Hoover cart.

NOTE: The opening words "Governor Cherry" referred to Governor R. Gregg Cherry of North Carolina. Later the president referred to former governor O. Max Gardner, Democratic candidate for governor W. Kerr Scott, and Democratic candidate for senator J. Melville Broughton, all of North Carolina.

OCTOBER 23

Address at Public Square Park

Wilkes-Barre, Pennsylvania (9:40 A.M.)

Thank you — thank you very much. I certainly appreciate most highly the cordial and friendly welcome of your distinguished mayor. He wonders how I stand the campaign! I will explain it to him.

When I was a very young man, I campaigned in the township to be township committeeman, and I failed to make the grade. When I got to be a little older, I campaigned in the county to be county judge, and I made that grade. Then on several occasions I campaigned through the whole state for senator, and of about 114 counties in the state I made them all.

Now, as president of the United States and head of the Democratic Party, it is my duty to let the people know just what I stand for and what the Democratic Party means. And when I have a duty to do, it is never too great to be done.

I certainly appreciate the privilege of meeting former Sergeant Hopkins, who was in the 109th Field Artillery. I did happen to be on the ridge at Mont Blaineville and fired on two German batteries. I didn't know I was doing anybody any good at that time. I just saw these batteries firing and put them out of commission. That sometimes happens in politics too.

It certainly is a pleasure to be in this wonderful city of Wilkes-Barre today. A Democrat ought to feel at home here, in a city and county which have supported the Democratic Party consistently — except for a little mistake in 1946!

We can't afford to make mistakes like that this year. This election is too important.

Just one fundamental issue in this election this time, and that is the people against the special interests. And when you vote at the polls on November 2, you will either vote for yourself or you will vote against yourself. Remember that.

I have been telling your neighbors over in Scranton what the Republican 80th Congress has done to labor and what the Republican Party plans to do to labor, if it gets control of the 81st Congress and puts a Republican president in the White House.

You know, I exercised my power of veto oftener than any other president of the United States in the time limit, except Grover Cleveland, and each of those vetoes I felt was in the public interest. Suppose I hadn't been there! The 80th Congress would have certainly fixed you sure enough, but they didn't have a chance to do all the things they wanted to do. All you have to do to avoid a mistake like the 80th Congress is to come out and vote on November 2.

Wilkes-Barre deserves to have a representative in Congress who will vote in the interest of the people who live here — in your interest. You ought to have a congressman who will vote to bring down high prices, to provide you with better Social Security, and good, decent, American homes. You deserve to have a Congressman who will vote for you and not against you. Don't make a mistake again. Send Dan Flood back to Congress where he belongs. He was a good congressman.

Your city of Wilkes-Barre is a perfect example of what has made this country the leading nation in the world today — the greatest nation in the world on which the sun has ever shone upon. The greatest nation in the world today is the United States of America, and Wilkes-Barre made this country great. It is named after two great fighters for human liberty — John Wilkes and Isaac Barre. Wilkes-Barre has grown because men and women who loved liberty have come here from all over the world. You have fought for human liberty too — in your businesses, in building up strong labor unions, and in the armed forces of this country, fighting for freedom throughout the whole world in two great wars. This is the real American way.

The ordinary common people of the world are just like we are. They want peace and security, and that is what we are trying to obtain for them. We know that the people of the world really want freedom and liberty. We understand the sufferings and struggles of those in the lands from which we came. We know that they want freedom, no matter what regime may be imposed upon them by force or treachery.

The Democratic Party stands for aid to people of other lands in their struggles against tyranny. We know that the people of the world really want liberty and freedom.

During the 80th Congress, one of the pieces of legislation in which I was most interested was the displaced persons bill. This bill opens the door to a portion of those former victims of Nazism, people from Poland, Lithuania, Latvia, Estonia, Czechoslovakia, Hungary, and other European countries who have been persecuted by Germans and who don't want to go back to tyranny behind the Soviet iron curtain.

I wanted to see our country admit its fair share of these helpless victims. I wanted to see them come in without any discrimination, but the Republican 80th Congress passed a law which discriminates against certain groups. It excludes nearly all displaced persons who belong to the Jewish faith, and it excludes an unfair proportion of those belonging to the Catholic faith. I don't think that is right. It is not American.

I asked the Republican Congress to change this law at the special session last July, but it refused to act. Now, if you want to see these displaced persons, who have so much in common with us, treated on a fair and equal basis, you have got to elect a Democratic Congress on November 2.

If you elect a Democratic Congress, you will be sure of getting laws which will help out all the people of the United States, and not just a powerful, wealthy few.

We need a law that will provide a half million units of low-rent public housing, clearance of slums, and rural housing. The Democratic Congress will give you that sort of law, because that is a part of the Democratic platform.

We need federal aid to education. The Democratic Congress will give you that aid, because that is a part of the Democratic platform.

We need a least a 75-cent minimum wage. The Democratic Congress will give us that minimum wage. Now the Republican candidate says he is for a minimum wage, and I think the sort he wants is the smaller the minimum the better.

We need extension of Social Security to everybody in the entire nation not now covered, and a 50 percent increase in benefits. A Democratic Congress will give us that extension and that increase. The Republicans said they are for Social Security, but when they had the power and the Congress, they took Social Security away from a million people that had it.

We need controls on inflation. A Democratic Congress, I think, will give us these controls.

I am urging you with everything I have to vote the Democratic ticket straight November 2, and then we can go on to build the kind of people's America that our great President Franklin D. Roosevelt had in mind when he gave us the New Deal. We can build the kind of prosperous nation we all want in a peaceful world that I want — and I am sure you want and need. Thank you very much.

NOTE: During his address the president referred to Mayor Luther M. Kniffen of Wilkes-Barre; former sergeant Robert Hopkins, Battery B, 109th Field Artillery; and former representative Daniel J. Flood of Pennsylvania.

OCTOBER 23

Address at the Hunt Armory

Pittsburgh (9 P.M.)

Mr. Chairman and fellow Democrats of Allegheny County:

I can't tell you how very much I appreciate this magnificent reception. I am always happy when I am with John Kane and Dave Lawrence and Frank Myers and all the rest of the good Democrats of Pennsylvania.

I think a presidential campaign is one of the most important elements in our democratic process. It's a chance to get things out in the open and discuss them and make decisions. I am an old campaigner, and I enjoy it. This is about my 230th meeting, and I am still going strong, and I will be going strong at midnight of November the 1st.

You know, I would enjoy this campaign a lot more if my opponent had the courage to discuss the issues. The American people have the right to know where I stand and where my opponent stands on the issues that affect every person in this country.

Now, the people know where I stand. But the Republican candidate refuses to tell where he stands. My opponent is conducting a very peculiar campaign. He has set himself up as some kind of doctor with a magic cure for all the ills of mankind.

Now, let's imagine that we, the American people, are going to see this doctor. It's just our usual routine checkup which we have every four years. Now, we go into this doctor's office. And, "Doctor," we say, "we're feeling fine."

"Is that so?" says the doctor. "You been bothered much by issues lately?"

"Not bothered, exactly," we say. "Of course, we've had a few. We've had the issues of high prices and housing and education and Social Security and a few others."

"That's too bad," says the doctor. "You shouldn't have so many issues."

"Is that right?" we say. "We thought that issues were a sign of political health."

"Not at all," says the doctor. "You shouldn't think about issues. What you need is my brand of soothing syrup — I call it 'unity.' "

Then the doctor edges up a little closer. And he says, "Say, you don't look so good."

We say to him, "Well, that seems strange to me, Doc. I never felt stronger, never had more money, and never had a brighter future. What is wrong with me?"

Well, the doctor looks blank, and he says, "I never discuss issues with a patient. But what you need is a major operation."

"Will it be serious, Doc?" we say.

"Not so very serious," he says. "It will just mean taking out the complete works and putting in a Republican administration."

Now, that's the kind of campaign you have been getting from the Republicans. They won't talk about the issues, but they insist that a major operation is necessary.

Take this vague talk of the Republican candidate about the "failures" of the present administration. That puzzled me for a little bit.

I thought of the fact that our national income is now running at the rate of over $220 billion a year — over five times as much as it was in 1932. Is that what he calls a failure?

Or perhaps he was worried about the profits of the corporations. In 1932, corporations lost $3 billion — lost $3 billion. Now corporate profits are running at the rate of $19 billion a year, after taxes. Is that what he calls a failure?

Perhaps he was thinking about our mighty undertakings to assist the free nations of the world to protect themselves against the inroads of communism. These efforts are proving successful. Is that what he calls a failure?

In his speech here in Pittsburgh just a few days ago, the Republican candidate pretended to be upset about the way my administration has treated labor — about the terrible condition that labor was in in 1946. That's the excuse he gives for the passage of the Taft-Hartley law. All right — all right, let's examine that.

In 1946 more people had jobs than ever before in the history of the country. Unions were healthier and had more members than ever before. And the workingmen and women of the United States produced more goods in 1946 than in any previous peacetime year.

The world wasn't perfect in 1946. But before any Republican begins complaining about that, he had better take a look at 1932 — the last Republican year. The Republican candidate talks about the workdays lost from strikes in 1946. Our industrial production in 1946 was three times as much as it was in 1932. And the days lost from strikes in 1946 were less than $1\frac{1}{2}$ percent of the total days worked that year.

Republicans don't like to talk about 1932 — and I don't blame them. Do you? But it is a good year for you to remember when you start out to vote on election day.

When the Republican candidate finished telling you, here in Pittsburgh, how labor had suffered under my administration, he told you who had come to the rescue of labor. Now, who do you think it was? It was the Republicans, according to the Republican candidate. Now, how do you suppose they did it? They did it with the Taft-Hartley Act. That is how they came to the rescue of labor.

Yes, sir. The Republican candidate marched up proudly and embraced the Taft-Hartley law — lock, stock, and barrel. No workingman can have any doubt about that anymore. And in praising the Taft-Hartley law, he displayed his characteristic tendency of claiming credit where no credit is due. He tried to tell you that it is the Taft-Hartley Act that is driving the Communists out of labor unions.

Now, if you want to know how much truth there is in this claim, ask Bill Green — ask Phil Murray. They will tell you who got the Communists out. It's being done in the good American way — the unions are doing it themselves.

Now, in this speech the Republican candidate made here in Pittsburgh, he admitted, with characteristic modesty, that he is going to lead the country — and, indeed, the whole world — out of all its troubles. And he made a lot of promises. He opened his mouth and he closed his eyes, and he swallowed the terrible record of that good-for-nothing Republican 80th Congress.

Now, four years ago this same Republican presidential candidate went around the country saying that he was in favor of what the Democrats had done, but he could do it better. He said he was in favor of the National Labor Relations Act, the Wage and Hour Act, the Social Security Act, and "all the other federal statutes designed to promote and protect the welfare of the American workingmen and women" — but he could do it better. For some reason or other the American people did not believe him in 1944.

This year the same candidate is back with us, and he is saying much the same thing; that he likes the Democratic laws but that he can run them better than we can. It sounds to me like the same old phonograph record; but this year the record has a crack, and the needle gets stuck in that crack every once in a while.

Now, the crack in the soothing syrup of that record was provided by the Republican 80th "do-nothing" Congress. Now, in 1948, every time the Republican candidate says, "I can do it better," up comes an echo from the crack which says, "We're against it." So the sounds coming out of the Republican Party this year are not very harmonious. And they are even less believable than they were in 1944.

The candidate said, and I quote: "The present minimum wage set by law is far too low and it will be raised." Now, that's fine. I am glad he said that. We're right with the candidate on that. In fact, we are way out ahead of him.

Time and time again in the last two years I urged the Republican "do-nothing" 80th Congress to raise the minimum wage from the present 40 cents an hour to at least 75 cents an hour. But that Republican Congress — that crack in the record — said, "Nothing doing — we're against it." And the minimum wage stayed where it was. Now, the Republicans like to say they are for a minimum wage, but it is perfectly clear that the smaller the minimum the better.

Now, let's look at another song on the record the candidate played for you here in Pittsburgh. That Republican candidate for president said, and I quote: "We will overhaul the Social Security system for the unemployed and the aged, and go forward to extend its coverage and increase its benefits." That is a direct quote from his speech, made right here in Pittsburgh. Now, that sounds good, although it's a little vague. But that's the candidate speaking. Where do the Republicans actually stand on Social Security?

As your president, I made every effort to get the Republican 80th Congress to extend Social Security coverage and increase Social Security benefits. What did the Congress do? They took Social Security benefits away from nearly a million people. What do you believe — campaign promises, or plain facts of Republican action? Now, again the cracked record gives them away. It says, "We're against it."

In my recommendations to the special "do-nothing" session of Congress in July, I pointed out the desperate need to increase old-age insurance benefits at least 50 percent. At the present time the average insurance benefit payment for an old couple is less than $40 a month. The Republican Congress did nothing about it — and neither did the Republican candidate for president. He was as silent as the tomb while the Congress was in session. Now, while he's campaigning, he suddenly takes quite an interest in increasing Social Security benefits. And I ask you: "Can you believe that kind of a campaign promise?"

That Republican outfit went to Philadelphia and wrote a platform, and that platform was the most hypocritical document that ever was written; and I called them back to Washington to see whether they meant what they said in their platform. And they didn't.

Take another promise in that Pittsburgh speech. The Republican candidate said, and I quote: "We will make the Labor Department equal in actual Cabinet status to Commerce and Agriculture. It will make an important contribution to the national welfare." Doesn't that sound nice?

That promise is ridiculous in the face of what the Republicans in the 80th Congress did. The Republican 80th Congress stripped the Mediation and Conciliation Service from the Labor Department. The Republican 80th Congress cut the appropriations for the Bureau of Labor Statistics almost in half — apparently to prevent the bureau from showing what's happening to the cost of living. That's the plain factual record of what the Republicans have done to the Labor Department in the last two years.

Remember, the Republican candidate has said he is proud of the record of the 80th Congress. But that crack in the record gives them away.

Here's another one of his promises. Here in Pittsburgh, the Republican candidate said, and I quote again: "We will bring a new and vigorous leadership to the Federal Conciliation and Mediation Service so that major disputes are settled before they become strikes."

Now, that's a very, very peculiar promise. The present director of the mediation service is a well-known industrial leader named Cyrus Ching. Mr. Ching has been widely praised for his work in mediation. I think the Republican candidate is a bit confused here. And that is not the only thing he is confused on, either.

Let me take another campaign promise, here in Pittsburgh. The Republican candidate said right here: "We will encourage unions to grow in responsibility and strengthen the processes of collective bargaining." I know it's hard to believe, but that's exactly what he said. And he said it in the very same speech in which he went all out for the Taft-Hartley law. Now, in this case, the candidate has fallen in the crack with the Republican Congress. He makes a promise, but the record says they're both against it.

Here's another promise by the Republican candidate; and I quote again: "We will vigorously and consistently enforce and strengthen our antitrust laws against business monopolies." Now, that's really fantastic. The Republican Party is notoriously favorable toward big business monopolies. The record of the Republican 80th Congress furnishes plenty of proof. They passed over my veto a bill to exempt railroads from antitrust laws. And at the same time they refused to pass, as I recommended, the O'Mahoney-Kefauver bill to plug loopholes in the antitrust laws.

In the face of that record, the candidate now claims that the Republicans will strengthen the antitrust laws. How can the Republican candidate say such things with a straight face?

But here's another — here's another! Here in Pittsburgh again, he said, and I quote: "We will break the logjam in housing so that decent houses may be provided at reasonable cost for the people."

For two solid years I tried in every way I knew to get the Republican 80th Congress to break the logjam in housing by passing the Taft-Ellender-Wagner bill. The Republicans would not act. In the face of pleading and urging from governors and mayors, from veterans and plain people all over the country, the Republican Congress refused to pass the housing bill. And I gave them four chances to do it. But now — now in the middle of the campaign — the Republican candidate has the gall to promise that the Republicans will take action on housing. I certainly wouldn't have believed it if I hadn't seen it in print.

Let me quote just one more campaign promise from the incredible Pittsburgh speech. "We will make sure," said the Republican candidate, I quote: "we will make sure that soaring prices do not steal food and clothing and other necessities from American families."

Now, that one completely stops me. Everybody in this country knows that the Republican 80th Congress refused, time and time again, to pass the laws we need to stop high prices. In November 1947, in January 1948, in July 1948, I asked that Republican Congress to act against inflation. They didn't do a thing about it.

And neither did the Republican candidate. All through the time when the Congress was in session, stalling and blocking anti-inflation legislation, the Republican candidate was as silent as the grave. But now — now that he's trying to persuade the people to vote for him — the Republican candidate says the Republicans will do something about high prices. It looks to me as though it's a little late in the game for that promise, anyway.

Now, the candidate says — the Republican candidate says: "Me, too." But the Republican record still says, "We're against it." And if you return the Republicans to power, you will have that same clique in control of the Congress that is in control of it now.

These two phrases — "Me, too" and "We're against it" — sum up the whole Republican campaign. My friends, it isn't funny at all. It's tragic, tragic for the everyday citizen.

This soft talk and double-talk, this combination of crafty silence and resounding misrepresentation, is an insult to the intelligence of the American voter. It proceeds upon the assumption that you can fool all the people — or enough of them — all the time.

In this campaign you don't have to rely on promises. This time, you have the record. You don't have to play just the Republican side of that record. Turn it over.

Our side — the Democratic side — doesn't say, "We're against it." It says, "We can do it." And we will do it — if you will give us a chance. Our side is the "Victory March" — a victory on November 2 for all the people and for the people's party — the Democratic Party.

NOTE: The opening words "Mr. Chairman" referred to John J. Kane, chairman of the Allegheny County Board of Commissioners. Later he referred to David L. Lawrence, mayor of Pittsburgh; Francis J. Myers, senator from Pennsylvania; William Green, president of the American Federation of Labor; Philip Murray, president of the Congress of Industrial Organizations; and Cyrus S. Ching, director of the Federal Mediation and Conciliation Service.

OCTOBER 24

Statement on Israel

The Republican candidate for president has seen fit to release a statement with reference to Palestine. This statement is in the form of a letter dated October 22, 1948, ten days before the election.

I had hoped our foreign affairs could continue to be handled on a nonpartisan basis without being injected into the presidential campaign. The Republican candidate's statement, however, makes it necessary for me to reiterate my own position with respect to Palestine.

I stand squarely on the provisions covering Israel in the Democratic platform. I approved the provisions on Israel at the time they were written. I reaffirm that approval now.

So that everyone may be familiar with my position, I set out here the Democratic platform on Israel:

> President Truman, by granting immediate recognition to Israel, led the world in extending friendship and welcome to a people who have long sought and justly deserve freedom and independence.

> We pledge full recognition to the State of Israel. We affirm our pride that the United States, under the leadership of President Truman, played a leading role in the adoption of the resolution of November 29, 1947, by the United Nations General Assembly for the creation of a Jewish state.

> We approve the claims of the State of Israel to the boundaries set forth in the United Nations' resolution of November 29 and consider that modifications thereof should be made only if fully acceptable to the State of Israel.

> We look forward to the admission of the State of Israel to the United Nations and its full participation in the international community of nations. We pledge appropriate aid to the State of Israel in developing its economy and resources.

We favor the revision of the arms embargo to accord to the State of Israel the right of self-defense. We pledge ourselves to work for the modification of any resolution of the United Nations to the extent that it may prevent any such revision.

We continue to support, within the framework of the United Nations, the internationalization of Jerusalem and the protection of the holy places in Palestine.

I wish to amplify the three portions of the platform about which there have been considerable discussion.

On May 14, 1948, this country recognized the existence of the independent State of Israel. I was informed by the Honorable Eliahu Epstein that a provisional government had been established in Israel. This country recognized the provisional government as the de facto authority of the new State of Israel. When a permanent government is elected in Israel, it will promptly be given de jure recognition.

The Democratic platform states that we approve the claims of Israel to the boundaries set forth in the United Nations resolution of November 29, 1947, and consider that modification thereof should be made only if fully acceptable to the State of Israel. This has been and is now my position.

Proceedings are now taking place in the United Nations looking toward an amicable settlement of the conflicting positions of the parties in Palestine. In the interests of peace this work must go forward.

A plan has been submitted which provides a basis for a renewed effort to bring about a peaceful adjustment of differences. It is hoped that by using this plan as a basis of negotiation, the conflicting claims of the parties can be settled.

With reference to the granting of a loan or loans to the State of Israel, I have directed the departments and agencies of the executive branch of our government to work together in expediting the consideration of any applications for loans which may be submitted by the State of Israel. It is my hope that such financial aid will soon be granted and that it will contribute substantially to the long-term development and stability of the Near East.

NOTE: On October 22, Thomas E. Dewey, Republican candidate for president, reaffirmed his position that the Jewish people were entitled to a homeland in Palestine. His views were expressed in a letter to Dean Alfange, chairman of the American Christian

Palestine Committee of New York. On January 25, 1949, a permanent government was elected in Israel, and on January 31 the White House announced that the United States had extended de jure recognition to the government of Israel. A summary of the United Nations resolution of November 29, 1947, providing for the partition of Palestine into independent Arab and Jewish states is printed in the *Department of State Bulletin*, vol. 17, p. 1163.

OCTOBER 25
Address at the Chicago Stadium
Chicago (9:04 P.M.)

Thank you, thank you very much. I can't tell you how very much I appreciate this most cordial Chicago welcome that no city in the world can equal.

It's a real pleasure to be here this evening in Illinois. One of the reasons for my special fondness for this great city is the memory of a man who was the last great governor, a distinguished Democrat and my friend. I refer, of course, to that great governor, Henry Horner. I hope that the people of Illinois will do all they can to bring back the same high ideals of government that he so much represented, in electing as your governor my good friend Adlai Stevenson. And if Illinois is to be properly represented in Washington, you'll want to elect to the Senate that able and outstanding liberal, Paul Douglas. While you're doing that, you might just as well elect the whole Democratic ticket here in Illinois.

I know you're going to pay tribute to Governor Horner's memory at the unveiling of a monument in Grant Park. I have always had the utmost admiration for Governor Horner, who was truly a great humanitarian. Racial and religious prejudice were unknown to him. He truly believed in the Fatherhood of God and the brotherhood of man. I sincerely regret that my schedule does not permit me to be here longer in person. You can be sure, however, that I will be here in spirit.

It is certainly inspiring to recall that in this hall, sixteen years ago, the Democratic Party gave the nation our great leader, Franklin D. Roosevelt. And when I think of Chicago, I can never forget that four years ago the Democratic Party honored me with the nomination for vice president of the

Before speaking at Chicago Stadium, Truman greeted Illinois gubernatorial nominee Adlai E. Stevenson. Former mayor Edward J. Kelly is between them and his successor, Martin H. Kennelly, is at Stevenson's right. (Cook County Democratic Central Committee)

United States, right here in this hall. There were 30 policemen getting me from the back of the hall to the platform. Tonight it took about 330.

We have passed through many stormy and exciting days since the election of 1944. We were fighting a terrible war then. We won that war for freedom, and we are now engaged in an even greater struggle — the struggle to preserve freedom and peace all over the world.

Now, the principal objective of my administration as president has been to create worldwide conditions of a just and lasting peace. I have never turned from that objective. And, my friends, I would much rather have peace in this world — a permanent peace in this world — than to be president of the United States or to hold any other office in the world. I have never turned from that objective. I never will stop working for peace.

I have worked hard for peace, because I know that peace is no idle dream. It is a real and living possibility. In our generation, mankind has taken some long steps toward this goal.

Thirty years ago, a great Democratic president gave voice to the conscience of the world when he proposed the League of Nations. The president — that great president — was Woodrow Wilson. Vicious partisan attacks kept the United States from joining the league, but Woodrow Wilson opened up a great vision for all those who have come after him.

Because we did not live up to our God-given opportunity, after World War I the League of Nations failed to prevent the most tragic war in history — World War II. I sincerely hope that we have learned that lesson.

Now we have another chance. We have a chance, this time, to build an enduring peace. We have that chance because of the vision of another great Democratic president. Franklin Roosevelt's wisdom and foresight inspired the nations of the world to forge a new and stronger instrument to keep the peace — the Charter of the United Nations. Today any nation that dares to contemplate aggressive war knows that it must face the collective judgment of the United Nations and the combined forces of many countries.

We all know that we have a long way to go before the threat of war is finally lifted. The United Nations still lacks much of the power which it must have to do its work successfully. But we are working to get that power for the United Nations, and eventually we will get it. We are on our way, and, please God, with courageous and sustained effort on the part of the free nations of the world, we can do more than merely avert war.

We can preserve for our children and our grandchildren the liberty and freedom which we enjoy today. We must do more than just avert war. We must also preserve here in the United States the kind of life we believe in and want to keep. That's why I am going to talk tonight about the attacks on our American democracy which are going on right now inside this country.

The American way of life which most of us have been taking for granted is threatened today by powerful forces of which most people are not even aware. Everybody knows about the contemptible Communist minority. We all detest that Communist minority. Everybody knows, too, about the crackpot forces of the extreme right wing. We have a vociferous representative of that force here in Chicago. We are on our guard against them, however.

The real danger to our democracy does not come only from these extremes. It comes mainly from the powerful reactionary forces which are silently undermining our democratic institutions. I am going to tell you just what these forces are.

We must not imagine, just because we love freedom, that freedom is safe — that our freedom is safe. Eternal vigilance is still the price of liberty.

Other people have also loved freedom but have lost their liberty with tragic suddenness. It happened in Italy twenty-five years ago. It happened in Germany fifteen years ago. It happened in Czechoslovakia just a few months ago. And it could happen here.

I know that it is hard for Americans to admit this danger. American democracy has very deep roots. But if the antidemocratic forces in this country continue to work unchecked, this nation could awaken a few years from now to find that the Bill of Rights had become a scrap of paper.

My friends, that must never happen! Look back over history, and you will find that wherever ruthless men have destroyed liberty and human rights, certain economic and social forces had paved the way for them.

What are these forces that threaten our way of life? Who are the men behind them? They are the men who want to see inflation continue unchecked. They are the men who are striving to concentrate great economic power in their own hands. They are the men who are setting up and stirring up racial and religious prejudice against some of our fellow Americans.

I propose to state in simple, unmistakable language, just exactly how each of these three groups of men — working through the Republican Party, if you please — is a serious threat to the future welfare of this great nation.

Let's take that first group — the men who want to see inflation continue unchecked. Believe it or not, there are such men. They know that inflation — since price controls were killed just over two years ago — has sent corporation profits soaring to the fantastic level of nearly $20 billion a year. They are so blinded by the glitter of gold that they forget that inflation — if it is not stopped — will bring on another terrible crash like the one of 1929.

We were fortunate to be led from that depression to new prosperity by a great and true lover of democracy — Franklin Roosevelt. But we cannot always count on being led — in time of economic trouble — by a man with genuine faith in the people. When people are hungry and homeless and frightened, they are easy victims for clever demagogues. In our own time, we have seen the tragedy of the Italian and German peoples, who lost their freedom to men who made promises of unity and efficiency and security.

I have had all this in mind in the long, hard fight I have been making on inflation. When I asked the Republican 80th Congress to pass laws to check inflation, I was thinking not only of high prices, not only of our housewives and the daily budget. I was thinking also of the urgent need to prevent another boom-and-bust cycle that would surely endanger our democracy.

When those Republican leaders of the 80th Congress failed to act against inflation, they proved themselves blind to the lessons of history. The American people cannot afford to entrust their future to men of such little vision. The Bible warns us that where there is no vision, the people perish. That is why I urge the election, on November the 2nd, of a Democratic Congress and a Democratic president.

We must never again entrust our political destinies to men who lack the will to safeguard our future and our freedoms. I say to you, if you want to protect American democracy, you must elect a Congress and an administration that will meet the peril of inflation squarely, and conquer it.

Now, the record conclusively proves that you cannot rely on the Republican Party to do that. The Democratic Party, and the Democratic Party alone, has led the fight on inflation.

Now, let's look at that group of men who are jeopardizing the future of democracy in the United States through their concentrated economic power. This is just as dangerous as inflation. Again and again in history, economic power concentrated in the hands of a few men has led to the loss of freedom.

When a few men get control of the economy of a nation, they find a "front man" to run the country for them. Before Hitler came to power, control over the German economy had passed into the hands of a small group of rich manufacturers, bankers, and landowners. These men decided that Germany had to have a tough, ruthless dictator who would play their game and crush the strong German labor unions. So they put money and influence behind Adolf Hitler. We know the rest of the story.

We also know that in Italy, in the 1920s, powerful Italian businessmen backed Mussolini and that, in the 1930s, Japanese financiers helped Tojo's military clique take over Japan.

Today, in the United States, there is a growing — and dangerous — concentration of immense economic power in the hands of just a few men. That's a dangerous situation. The Democratic Party has been fighting that ever since the Democratic Party has been in existence. This 80th Congress I talk so much about was the tool of that sort of a situation in this country. They contributed towards the concentration of wealth.

Great corporations have been expanding their power steadily. They have been squeezing small business further and further out of the picture. The lobbies which work for big business found that they could get what their bosses wanted from the Republican leaders of the 80th Congress. That 80th Congress was beset by more lobbyists and more powerful lobbyists than any Congress in the history of these United States.

Now, my friends, the record of that 80th Congress is a sad tale of the sellout of the people's interest to put more and more power into the hands of fewer and fewer men. The Republican Congress, acting for big business, has already begun its attack to break the strength of labor unions by voting the vicious Taft-Hartley law. I vetoed that bill and fought to prevent its passage with all the strength I had as president of the United States. That Taft-Hartley law is the opening gun in the Republican onslaught against the rights of the workingmen in this country.

The Republican 80th Congress repeatedly flouted the will of the people. And yet the Republican candidate has the gall to say, and I quote him verbatim: "The 80th Congress delivered as no other Congress ever did for the future of this country."

Well, I'll say it delivered. It delivered for the private power lobby. It delivered for the big oil company lobby. It delivered for the railroad lobby. It delivered for the real estate lobby. That's what the Republican candidate calls delivering for the future. Is that the kind of future you want? Well, I'm sure you don't, so be sure you elect a Democratic president and a Democratic Congress on November 2.

In the last two years, I have had to use my veto power time and again on major pieces of legislation to prevent the Republican Congress from turning the country upside down and shaking out its pockets. The actions of the Congress lead to one inescapable conclusion — Republican leaders stand ready to deliver to big business more and more control over the resources of this nation and the rights of the American people.

In 1933 the Democratic Party drove the money changers out of the temple and brought new life to our democracy. Now, this Republican Party is making soap-bubble promises to behave better in the future. Those bubbles are pretty, those promises are fine, but they will vanish at the first touch of reality. You cannot expect the Republican Party suddenly to turn and bite the hand that has been feeding it — the hand of the special interests and the hand of big business.

To preserve freedom and democracy in this country, we must put control of the Congress back in the hands of the American people. This means we must have a Democratic Congress and a Democratic president.

Now, I must speak of the third evil force which works secretly to destroy freedom — racial and religious prejudice. The tragic story of what happened in Germany is all too fresh. We know how Hitler used anti-Semitic propaganda as a way of stupefying the German people with false ideas while he reached out for power. This was not the first time such a thing has happened. The persecution of minorities goes hand in hand with the destruction of liberty.

This country has been mercifully spared extreme racial and religious strife. But in recent years there has been a new outcropping of demagogues among us. Dangerous men, who are trying to win followers for their war on democracy, are attacking Catholics and Jews and Negroes and other minority races and religions.

Some of these demagogues have even dared to raise their voice of religious prejudice in the 80th Congress. We need only remember the shocking displaced persons bill passed in the second session of the 80th Congress, which cruelly discriminated against Catholics and Jews.

We must do everything we can to protect our democratic principles against those who foment racial and religious prejudice. This evil force must be defeated. I shall continue the fight. And I pledge to you that I shall never surrender.

Racial and religious oppression, big-business domination, inflation — these forces must be stopped and driven back while there is yet time. At any cost, we must prevent the threatened depression and the big-business rule which would begin the destruction of our liberties. We must continue the fight to assure full human rights to all our citizens.

Now, my friends, the Democratic Party is the only party which the people can rely on to serve these great ends. Republican leaders, of course, give lip service to the principles of democracy. But the Republicans preach one thing and practice another. The actions of the Republican 80th Congress opened the gate to forces that would destroy our democracy. The gate is open just a little bit right now. We need to slam that gate shut on November 2 with an overwhelming vote for the Democratic Party.

Now, you people here in Chicago have a clear-cut example of the difference between Democratic and Republican concepts of government. The whole country recognizes that the Democratic administration of Chicago is doing a grand job. It is providing first-rate local government. And the whole country knows, also, that the Republican administration of this state has been reactionary, feeble, and opposed to every forward piece of legislation. Such is the spirit behind government by Republicans in this great state. In that spirit, democracy can be destroyed and tyranny born.

That is why I say to you that we are now engaged in one of the most important battles in our history. It is a crusade for the right, a crusade for the people against the special interests. I want you to join me in this crusade. This is not just a battle between two parties. It is a fight for the very soul of the American government.

The facts show the Republican Party is unwilling to check inflation and has sponsored repressive labor legislation. The facts show that the Republican Party is working today, as it worked throughout most of its history, to deliver this country into the hands of the special interests and big business.

In this battle, the independent voters of the United States will decide the issue. By throwing their weight to the Republicans or the Democrats, they will choose the forces which are to compose our government.

Day by day, ever since this campaign began, more and more independent American voters have been lining up with the Democratic Party. They have learned the facts, and the only way they could learn those facts was to learn them from the president of the United States; and I have talked to more than six million people in this United States, and they know the facts now. They are determined to sweep back the forces that threaten democracy in this country.

All over the nation, I have seen unmistakable evidence that the American people are waking up to the tremendous issues which confront them in this election. We are sweeping toward victory, my friends. Everywhere I go, I hear news and see faces that make me know the tide is rolling for us. In the next few days, it is going to roll even higher. With your help, your unflagging courage — with your enthusiasm in a great cause, we are going to win this election on November the 2nd.

NOTE: During his address he referred to former governor Henry Horner, Democratic candidate for governor Adlai E. Stevenson, and Democratic candidate for senator Paul H. Douglas, all of Illinois. The address was carried on a nationwide radio broadcast.

★ ★ ★ ★ ★ ★ ★ ★ ★ ★ ★ ★ ★ ★ ★ ★ ★

OCTOBER 26

Address at the Cleveland Municipal Auditorium
Cleveland (9 P.M.)

Thank you, thank you — thank you very, very much. I can't tell you how very much I appreciate that reception. I want to say to you tonight, Mr. Chairman and ladies and gentlemen — I am going to let you in on a secret. We have got the Republicans on the run.

Of course, the Republicans don't want to admit that. They've got a poll that says they're going to win.

Well, we all know that for twelve years the Republicans have been poll-happy. In 1936 the Republicans had a poll that told them they had a sure thing. And they did. They met a sure defeat in 1936!

In 1940 the Republicans had a poll that told them they had the edge. Well, it was a mighty sharp edge. They got cut to ribbons on election day, if you remember.

In 1944 — you know that on that ticket in 1944 the Republicans had a poll that told them things were pretty close. It looked mighty promising for the Republican candidate, so the poll said. Now, that promise was all he got. In fact, the Republicans have been full of promises ever since.

This year the Republicans have some polls right down the same old line. The Republican candidate is putting out polls. These polls that the Republican candidate is putting out are like sleeping pills designed to lull the voters into sleeping on election day. You might call them sleeping polls.

You know that the same doctor I told you about in Pittsburgh the other night — that Republican candidate — keeps handing out these sleeping polls, and a lot of people have been taking them. The doctor keeps telling the people: "Don't worry. Take a poll and go to sleep."

Most of the people are not going to be lulled to sleep or be fooled. They know that sleeping polls are bad for the system. They affect the mind and the body. An overdose could be fatal — can so affect your mind that your body will be too lazy to go to the polls on election day. "You don't need to vote; the election is won — all I have to do is get Truman out of the White House."

Now, these Republican polls are no accident. They are part of a design to prevent a big vote, to keep you at home on November 2 by convincing you that it makes no difference whether you vote or not.

They want to do this because they know in their hearts that a big vote spells their defeat. They know that a big vote means a Democratic victory, because the Democratic Party stands for the greatest good for the greatest number of the people. The special interests now running the Republican Party can't stand a big vote — they are afraid of the people.

My friends, we are going to win this election, because the people believe what the Democrats stand for — they also know too well what the Republicans stand for. And, believe me, the Republicans and the Democrats do not stand for the same thing. You can tell that very plainly by looking at the candidates you have to vote for here in Cleveland.

Just consider the man who will be your next governor — Frank Lausche. Frank Lausche is a man of the people, who, like Cleveland's great mayors Tom Johnson and Tom Burke, thinks with his heart as well as with his head.

This is a state of great Democrats — honest, able, fearless men — senior statesmen like my friend Bob Crosser here, and the younger men worthy to fight at their side, like Steve Young, who is going to be your congressman at large. Men like Mike Kirwan, the chairman of the Congressional Campaign Committee, whose work to assure the election of a Democratic Congress will never be forgotten in the history of the Democratic Party. Men like your own great Mike Feighan and like Walter Huber.

The Republicans can't win against candidates like these men when the people get out and vote. They can't win with a candidate for president who dodges the issues, either.

The American people want to know what kind of government they can expect from the men and women they elect to office. And thanks to the record that has been made, this is one time the voters can tell just what to expect.

The record of the Democratic Party is blazed across the face of the nation in a story of a better, healthier, happier life for all Americans. The Democratic record is a record of performance and not a record of false promises.

The record of the Republican Party was a story of obstruction, objection, and reaction from the days of the Hoover depression to the end of the 80th Congress. And then there came a faint ray of hope — a suggestion that the Republican Party might mend its ways. In June of 1948 the Republican Party wrote its platform in Philadelphia. That platform failed to mention many of the issues, but it almost caught up with the Democratic platform of 1932.

Now, for two long years I had been urging the Republican Congress to do something about high prices and housing and to bring Social Security and the other welfare measures up to date. All this time, the situation had been getting worse. Prices had become unbearable for most people. Now, in this 1948 platform, the Republican Party had indicated that it might be willing to do something.

Encouraged by this platform, I called a special session of the 80th Congress. The Republicans had a chance to promise in Philadelphia. And I gave them a chance to perform in Washington. I did this because I believe that it is the president's job to get decent laws for the benefit of the American people and because the people were demanding action.

Seldom in history has a party had such an opportunity to show good faith by converting its platform promises into legislative performance. But did the Republicans take advantage of that opportunity? They did not. They cared nothing about their platform promises or for the legislation which was so urgently needed for the public good.

Let me remind you what the Republicans said when they found out what my recommendations were. The Republican leaders issued an official statement, and this is what it said: "The president's quarrel with the 80th Congress is not the failure to enact legislation but a fundamental difference in government philosophy between the president and the Congress."

I am going to read you that quote again, because that is of vital importance in this campaign: "The president's quarrel with the Congress — with the 80th Congress, is not its failure to enact legislation but a fundamental difference in government philosophy between the president and the Congress."

To put it in plain English, it means that I believe in one kind of government: government for the people. The Republicans believe in another kind of government: government for special interests.

Now, the question in this election is — which of these two kinds of government do you want? Do you want government for all the people, or do you want government for the privileged few?

Let's get one thing clear. When the Republican leaders made their statement, they had already picked their candidate for president. That candidate stands for the same fundamental philosophy as that Republican "do-nothing" 80th Congress does. Now, just in case there was ever any doubt about that, the Republican candidate has since indorsed the record of that 80th Congress.

But all the while the Republican 80th Congress was in session, that candidate was very, very quiet, about it. And although he has said he is proud of the record of the 80th Congress, he has been trying to make us forget what that Congress actually did and failed to do. He has treated it like a poor relation; he shut it up in the back room, so that its bad manners and terrible record won't frighten the voters he is entertaining in the front parlor. And the reason is that, in everything it said and did, the Republican 80th Congress showed exactly what the difference is between the Republican kind of government and the Democratic kind of government.

And it is my duty to make that difference perfectly clear, and that is what I am trying to do for you. The best way I know of doing that is to explain what I asked the special session of the 80th Congress to do.

I know this is going to be painful to the Republican candidate. He is having such a high-level tea party with the voters that he is horrified whenever anybody mentions the facts of life.

Here I am proposing to drag the old reprobate of a Republican 80th Congress out of the back room and disclose him to the guests as the candidate's nearest and dearest relative. I'm going to tell the folks exactly how I gave that old sinner a chance to repent in the special session. I gave him a chance to mend his ways — only three weeks after he had taken the pledge at Philadelphia — and how he refused and backslid again into the gutter of special privilege.

The Republican Party can change platforms and candidates, but it can't change its fundamental philosophy of government. If you believe in the things I recommended to the special session of the 80th Congress, you must vote the Democratic ticket straight.

My first recommendation to the special session of that Congress was for effective action to hold down high prices. But this was contrary to the fundamental Republican philosophy. It would have interfered with the excessive profits of the big corporations. So the Republicans are against it.

I'm still in favor of action to hold down the cost of living, and I believe that you are. And if that is what you want, you can get it by voting the straight Democratic ticket on election day.

The second recommendation I made to the special session was for the passage of the Taft-Ellender-Wagner Housing Bill. This bill had already passed the Senate and would have passed the House within an hour if the Republican leaders had permitted it to come to a vote. But the real estate lobby wanted it blocked, so the masters of the Republican Party blocked it.

This is their fundamental philosophy on housing, and I'm glad it's different from mine. This question is going to be before you on election day just as plainly as if it were on your ballot. And to get housing for the masses, you must vote the Democratic ticket on November 2.

If you are for slum clearance, if you are for government aid for housing at reasonable prices, if you are for immediate action in the people's interest — you must vote the Democratic ticket.

Now, let's look at the next question I put up to them. That's federal aid to education. I don't have to tell you how crowded the schools are and how much we need more classrooms and more teachers at better salaries. This is a matter of national concern. And I have urged that the Congress help the states in meeting the present crisis. It is certainly a disgrace on the richest country in the world not to have rooms enough for its children to go to school, and to be so picayune with the teachers that they can't afford to teach in the schools for the pay they get.

Here again, a bill had already passed the Senate and could have passed the House very quickly. And here again the masters of the Republican Party refused to let the representatives of the people even vote on this vital matter. That's the kind of efficiency you get from the Republican Party. And they are always talking about efficiency!

It seems incredible that the Republicans should admit that their fundamental philosophy requires them to oppose adequate schools — but admit it they did. With them, money comes ahead of schools.

Remember, you will be voting for or against better schools, more teachers at better pay, on election day. And if you want better schools, more teachers at better pay, you must vote the Democratic ticket.

Then I gave this special session a chance to raise the minimum wage. It's only 40 cents an hour now. Suppose some of these Republican congressmen had to try to raise a family on $16 a week. Maybe they would change their minds about the minimum wage.

But, as of last July 28, a higher minimum wage was contrary to the fundamental philosophy of the Republican Party. Their candidate says he is for a minimum wage, but I have come to the conclusion that the smaller the minimum, the better it will suit him. Now, to raise that minimum wage, you have got to vote the Democratic ticket on November the 2nd.

I asked the Congress to do something else too. Oh, I gave them a number of chances. I asked them to increase the Social Security insurance payments. The average payment to an old couple is less than $40 a month. That's a pitifully inadequate sum to try to live on, isn't it? But it's enough to satisfy the fundamental Republican philosophy.

In fact, if you judge the Republicans by their actions and not their campaign promises, they are opposed to Social Security altogether. The kind of action the Republican 80th Congress took was to strip Social Security insurance benefits from nearly a million people who already had them.

If you don't want to take a chance on having your Social Security benefits whittled away, you had better vote the Democratic ticket on November the 2nd.

Now, there was something else I asked this special session to do. That was to correct an injustice this same Republican 80th Congress had perpetrated at its regular session.

The Congress passed a displaced persons bill at the regular session which discriminated against Jews and Catholics. This display of intolerance aroused such a storm of protest from all fair-minded people that I thought the Republicans might be glad of a chance to correct the injustice they had done to the good people of those two faiths. I gave them that chance. Did they use it? They did not.

This was one question on which the Republican candidate felt he couldn't afford to keep silent. So he asked the Republicans in Congress to act. And what did they do? They told him who was really riding the elephant. Now, if that's unity, I don't know unity when I see it. And that is what the Republican candidate is asking for.

I gave them a chance to correct another wrong, too. Oh, I was as generous as I could be with that Republican special session!

Earlier, at the regular session, when they had acted on appropriations for electric power projects, they had really messed up our national power policy. They had made so many cuts in funds, and included so many restrictions, that a severe power shortage is likely to result in many sections of the country. They even refused funds for the Tennessee Valley Authority to build a steam plant to help furnish power needed for our work on atomic energy.

I thought they would be glad of a chance to correct this mistake. But no, sir. They must have consulted their Republican candidate for president and learned his view that the TVA is wonderful, but we ought never to do anything like it again.

Finally, I urged the special session to act on legislation to protect the basic rights of citizenship and human liberty. The Republican Party has been paying lip service to legislation for this purpose for many years. But when the showdown comes, they never quite manage to act upon it.

The performance of this "do-nothing" 80th Congress during the past two years, and particularly the "do less than nothing" special session, has given the country a foretaste of what will happen if the Republican Party is successful at the polls.

The people of Ohio, particularly the residents of Cleveland, will long remember 1932, when the Republican Party was in power. Many of you can remember the smokeless smokestacks, the idle plants, the closed banks, the long breadlines, the soup kitchens. You can also remember the assurance you received from the Republicans that prosperity was just around the corner.

Now, it was the Democratic Party that lifted the nation from the worst depression it has ever known, under the leadership of Franklin D. Roosevelt. It was the Democratic Party that inspired and inaugurated a program of social legislation that restored democratic government to its proper place as the servant of the people and not the agent of the privileged few.

The Democratic Party stands ready to serve the nation — ready to serve all citizens and not just the vested interests, ready to carry on its "fundamental philosophy" that has done so much for the people of the United States in the last sixteen years.

Now, during the last two years, the Democratic Party has had to spend most of its time and energy in saving the Democratic program — the New Deal — from the Republican attacks upon it. As Democrats, we don't like this. We feel it is a bad thing to spend so much time preventing the Republicans from turning the clock back. We would much rather have the clock go along and go forward. And I would like to go forward with it.

Now, what this country needs is not a new president. What this country needs is a new Congress — a Democratic Congress. Now, all I am asking you to do is to go to the polls on November the 2nd and vote for yourselves. Vote in your own interests. If you do that, you will have a Democratic administration here in the great state of Ohio, you will have a Democratic president in the White House, and you will have a Democratic Congress that will be willing to serve the people and not the special interests.

NOTE: In his opening words the president referred to Ray T. Miller, chairman of the Cuyahoga County Democratic Executive Committee. Later he referred to Democratic candidate for governor Frank J. Lausche, Mayor Thomas A. Burke of Cleveland, former mayor Thomas Johnson of Cleveland, Democratic candidate for representative Stephen M. Young, and Representatives Robert Crosser, Michael J. Kirwan, Michael A. Feighan, and Walter B. Huber, all of Ohio.

★ ★ ★ ★ ★ ★ ★ ★ ★ ★ ★ ★ ★ ★ ★ ★

OCTOBER 28

Address at Madison Square Garden
New York City (10:34 P.M.)

Thank you very much. Thank you. It is certainly good to be here tonight. You know, I was here four years ago on the same errand. It's always a pleasure to come to this great city — especially when you have so many friends.

But there is a special reason why I am glad to be here tonight. New York is a mighty source of strength in the battle we are waging to preserve liberal government in the United States. It is the birthplace of many liberal and progressive programs which have restored the strength of the nation during the last sixteen years. It is the state of those true Democrats and great Americans Al Smith, Bob Wagner, Herbert Lehman, and, above all, Franklin Roosevelt. It was here in this state that these men did so much to give new life and new meaning to the principles of democracy. And when I say "democracy," I mean democracy as we understand it in this country. Because of their great work our country, and the entire world, is a better place in which to live.

We have come here tonight to this great gathering under the banner of the Liberal Party — a party which has done so much for liberal causes. And I consider it an honor to be here with the Liberal Party under that banner.

We have come here tonight with one mind and one purpose. We have come to pledge once more our faith in liberal government and to place in firm control of our national affairs those who believe with all their hearts in the principles of Franklin D. Roosevelt.

Now, I have a confession to make to you here tonight. For the last two or three weeks I've had a queer feeling that I'm being followed, that someone is following me. I felt it so strongly that I went into consultation with the White House physician. And I told him that I kept having this feeling, that everywhere I go there's somebody following behind me. The White House physician told me not to worry. He said: "You keep right on your way. There is one place where that fellow is not going to follow you — and that's in the White House."

I think the doctor's right. I'm going to be there, working for the people, for four more years because you believe that I'm trying to do the right thing.

Now, there are some other places besides the White House where this gentleman won't follow me. He won't follow me if I go into the record of the Democratic and Republican parties.

The Republican candidate can follow me all the way from Los Angeles to Madison Square Garden, but the Republican record makes it certain that he will still be trailing along behind when the votes are counted. He is doing all he can to make you forget that record. He doesn't dare talk about it. I have never in my life been in a campaign where the opposition refused absolutely to discuss the issues of the campaign. I can't understand that sort of an approach. But after I had analyzed the situation, I came to the conclusion that the record of the Republican Party is much too bad to talk about. The Republican candidate is trying to run on the record of the Democratic Party — of Franklin Roosevelt and myself. He's a "me, too" man.

Let's take a look at the record and see why he can't talk about the record of the Republican Party. Let's go back a few years. In 1928 the Republicans elected a well-known efficiency engineer named Herbert Hoover, and they promised us everything. They told us if we wanted prosperity, we must vote for Hoover. Well, the people fell for it. And I think this new candidate — well, he's not a new candidate — I think this secondhand candidate thinks the same way. You know what a bitter experience you had after that.

Many of you here tonight remember 1932. Over in Central Park, men and women were living in little groups of shacks made of cardboard and old boxes. They were known as "Hoovervilles." Out here on Eighth Avenue, veterans were selling apples. Ragged individualism — I suppose that's what you would call it. Farm foreclosures, homeowners' evictions, starvation wages, labor unions disrupted by company spies and thugs — that was the Republican record when they last had control of the government. And, you know, there is a peculiar thing about this campaign. I have never heard of a single Republican candidate for office point with pride to any Republican administration or any Republican president.

Now, they made an awful mess of things when they had control back there when they were elected in 1928. And in 1932 we turned them out. The vigorous action which saved the nation and restored our faith came with the Democrats, with the New Deal, and with Franklin Roosevelt.

We saved the banks. Now, in the last three years there hasn't been a single bank failure in the United States. We saved industry. Now, industry last year and this year have made the biggest profits they ever made in the history of the country — $17 billion last year, and nearly $20 billion this year. That's profits after taxes. We saved the insurance companies. We saved the railways.

At that point the Republicans said we had done enough. But we went right on saving this great nation of ours. We saved the people — the farmers, the workers, the unemployed, the old people who had lost their savings, and the young people who had never had a chance. And while we were at it, we saved the United States of America. We replanted the forests; we began soil conservation; we built great dams; we developed whole river valleys. We built roads and bridges, schoolhouses and courthouses. We built sidewalks and sewers, parks and playgrounds, and low-rent housing — and quite a few battleships too.

And all the time, the Republicans kept moaning that we were going too far. I was in the Senate during those years, and I heard them moaning. And the *Congressional Record* is the best evidence of the policies that the Republicans wanted to pursue, but they couldn't do it. They said we were undermining our own moral fiber — we were destroying individual initiative — that Roosevelt was a dictator, that we were opposed to free enterprise. Now, as early as 1936 they began saying that we were communistic and socialistic, red, or radical — because we cared for the people, and people knew it and liked it. They tried to scare labor in 1936 — you all remember this — by stuffing pay envelopes with propaganda against Social Security. That didn't work. They tried a new line of propaganda in 1940, and again it didn't work. The people knew better. They broke with tradition and chose Roosevelt for a third term.

World War II had come, and the country was in danger. But that meant nothing to Republican leadership. They came within a single vote in the Congress of the United States of disbanding our Army three months before Pearl Harbor — and they spent thousands of dollars and time, without stint, trying to prove that Pearl Harbor was brought about by one of greatest presidents who ever sat in the White House — and it's all turned out to be a pack of lies! They hindered and delayed our efforts to rearm the nation. Nobody knows more about that than I do, for I was there watching them.

And all the time they kept moaning and groaning that the New Deal had weakened America. Weakened America — think of that! Now, Tojo and Hitler knew better than that. They knew the answer to that one, even if the Republicans don't. But the Republicans kept on trying to stop us, trying to stop the people, and trying to kill the New Deal.

In 1944 the Republicans tried to talk their way into power again. They nominated a man who was violently opposed to the New Deal. In fact, he wrote a book about it. They nominated the same man they nominated this year — that's the reason I said he was a secondhand candidate. He was saying the same things in 1944 that he is saying today. He was attacking Franklin Roosevelt's administration then, and he is attacking my administration now. He says that because I want to talk about these things and because I want to talk about the issues that I'm just an ordinary political mudslinger. When I got out to the people of the United States, in every corner of the United States, in nearly every state of the Union, and told them what the facts are — then I'm a mudslinger. He can't stand the facts — that's what the trouble is.

Time and again in 1944 he told the voters that what we need is "strength and unity." He promised to displace — and I quote — "a tired, exhausted, quarreling, and bickering administration with a fresh and vigorous administration." Now, doesn't that sound familiar to you? And he asked, and I quote again: "Is the New Deal, the tired and quarrelsome New Deal, all America has to offer?" "Must we go back," he asked, "must we go back to leaf raking and doles?" Well, you people stuck by the New Deal in 1944, and we haven't had to go back to leaf raking or the doles or anything else of that kind. And the reason we haven't had to go back to Hooverville and breadlines and soup kitchens is because the Democratic policies of the New Deal are correct and right, and they're for all the people and not just for the privileged few.

I must say, though, that some of you are partly to blame for this, because you didn't vote in 1946. That Republican "do-nothing" 80th Congress did all it could to start us back down that dismal road.

Here's another one. At Baltimore just before the 1944 election, the Republican candidate said: "We must have a president who can and will work with Congress." He said he "would like to start the largest housecleaning Washington ever had." That sounds familiar, too, doesn't it? Now, he is playing the same old record again, and the record is stuck in the same old groove. What a wonderful thing it was for the people of this United States that they didn't have a president who would go along with that good-for-nothing 80th Congress! Now, he was speaking of the wartime administration of one of the greatest men in history, who was leading a united people to victory in the greatest war of all time. Roosevelt believed in the people, and the people believed in Roosevelt — and so did I. Even with millions of men overseas and away from their homes, the Roosevelt ticket won in 1944. Let me put it differently: the Republicans lost and the people won again in 1944.

You know what happened then. We won the war in the most complete military victory ever recorded in history. And since that war we have enjoyed the greatest peacetime prosperity in our history.

My friends, that's the record. And as Al Smith said, "If you look at the record, you can't go wrong." The record of Republican failure and Democratic success — that's why the Republican candidate won't follow me when I talk about the record.

There's another place also where he won't follow me. He won't follow me in discussing the issues of this campaign.

He can follow me into Framingham, Massachusetts, but he won't follow me in raising the minimum wage to at least 75 cents an hour. He said in this campaign that he is for a minimum wage — and I think the smaller the minimum, the better it suits him.

He can follow me into Cleveland, but he won't follow me and broaden the coverage of our Social Security insurance laws and increase their benefits by 50 percent. You know, an old couple now only gets $40 a month, and that's mighty little, just like that minimum wage — $16 a week. I've said time and again around the country that I wish that the Republican congressmen could have to live in Washington for a while on $16 a week or $40 a month. I think they would change their minds just a little bit.

He can follow me into Chicago, but he won't follow me in demanding that Congress pass laws for health insurance and medical care. You know, it's a shame and a disgrace that a country as rich and as important as this great country is today — the leader of all the world — is not able to give the people in the middle the proper kind of medical care. I've asked for health insurance because health insurance is the answer to a healthy nation — and someday we're going to get it.

He can follow me into Boston, but he won't follow me in calling for federal aid to education so that teachers can get a living wage and so that modern schools can be built and so that our children can get a decent education. That's another disgrace on this great country. And our Republican opponent has said that the teachers lobby — he called it "the Teachers Organization" — he's trying to work against the teachers lobby. He says it's the most vicious thing in this country — vicious because the teachers want to get a living wage and because they want to get decent housing for our schoolchildren! Now, we give money to the states to build roads. Why can't we also give money to the states from the federal government to build schoolhouses and pay teachers? I think it's much more important to see that the children that ride in the buses over these roads get the proper kind of schooling and the proper sort of teachers than it is to build the roads, myself. He doesn't go along with me on that.

He can follow me to Pittsfield and Providence, but when he gets there, they needn't expect him to give them any help on low-cost housing. You know, low-cost houses have been before the Congress for three years. It passed the Senate twice. First it was the Wagner-Ellender-Taft bill. That was killed. And then they introduced a new bill in the 80th Congress, and they called it the Taft-Ellender-Wagner bill. And when it came up for consideration the Republican leadership in the House of Representatives wouldn't even let it in, and the members of Congress in the lower house couldn't even vote on it; and when it came back for reconsideration in the Senate, Mr. Taft ran out on his own bill. I don't understand that.

He can follow me into New York City — and I wouldn't be surprised if he followed me right here into Madison Square Garden — but he won't follow me in demanding the repeal of the Taft-Hartley law. You can be sure of that. He can follow me right up here on this platform next Saturday night, but he won't follow me in calling for a law to control high prices. You can be sure of that.

On all these issues, when it comes to doing something for the people, the Republican candidate won't follow me — you can be sure of that. Sometimes it looks as if he is almost persuaded to follow me on some of these questions, but that's as far as he goes, and that, ladies and gentlemen, is as far as he's going to go. Because every time the Republican candidate looks at the program of the Democratic Party, he says, "Me, too," and his party's record says, "Nothing doing." And his party's record speaks louder than he does. You know, he is trying to persuade the people at large in the country that the elephant's got the new look, but it's just the same old elephant — you can be sure of that.

He could follow me all over the country in his campaign special, but he couldn't get his party to follow me and support a decent law for displaced persons.

Now, he couldn't get the old elephant to behave before election time, and I wonder how in the world he's going to get it to behave after election time with that same old leadership in the Congress. He can't do it.

Now, let me say in all seriousness that I am glad the Republican candidate has followed me around over the country, because it has shown the people how little he has to offer them. And the American people are not going to be fooled. They want to hear something more than platitudes. You know, "G.O.P." now stands for "Grand Old Platitudes."

The Republican candidate can follow me to every city, town, and village in this country. But so long as he is afraid to tell where he stands on the issues, he will lose more votes than he gains. Some of those Republican papers now are getting a little scared. They agree I might win. Don't you worry about that — I will win! A Democratic victory is on the way and he is doing all he can to help us win it, and I'm glad of that.

I wish to speak now upon a subject that has been of great interest to me as your president. It is the subject of Israel. Now, this is a most important subject and must not be resolved as a matter of politics during a political campaign. I have refused consistently to play politics during a political campaign. I have refused consistently to play politics with that question. I have refused, first, because it is my responsibility to see that our policy in Israel fits in with our foreign policy throughout the world; second, it is my desire to help build in Palestine a strong, prosperous, free, and independent democratic state. It must be large enough, free enough, and strong enough to make its people self-supporting and secure.

As president of the United States, back in 1945, I was the first to call for the immediate opening of Palestine to immigration to the extent of at least one hundred thousand persons. The United States, under my administration, led the way in November 1947 and was responsible for the resolution of the United Nations setting up Israel, not only as a homeland but as a free and independent political state. The United States was the first to give full and complete recognition to the new state of Israel in April 1948 and recognition to its provisional government.

I have never changed my position on Palestine or Israel. As I have previously announced, I have stood — and still stand — on the present Democratic platform of 1948. The platform of 1944 had provisions in it under which I have been trying to act. The platform of 1948 reiterates those positions and goes a little further — and I am glad it did go a little further. What we need now is to help the people of Israel — and they have proved themselves worthy of the best traditions of hardy pioneers. They have created out of the barren desert a modern and efficient state, with the highest standards of Western civilization. They have demonstrated that Israel deserves to take its place in the family of nations.

That is our objective. We shall work toward it, but we will not work toward it in a partisan and political way. I am confident that the objective will be reached. I know that no American citizen, of whatever race or religion, would want us to deal with the question of Palestine on any other basis than the welfare of all Americans of every race and faith.

That is the spirit in which all liberals face the issues of this campaign. We are concerned with justice, and we are deeply concerned with human rights — here in America as well as in the rest of the world.

I am happy to say to you tonight that the spirit of liberalism is going to triumph at the polls on November 2, just as sure as you are sitting in this hall.

The forces of reaction gained a beachhead in 1946 when they elected a Republican Congress. And this year they have redoubled their efforts to take over control of your government. And it is your government when you exercise the right to vote. And when you don't exercise the right to vote, you can't complain when such things as the 80th Congress come along and commence doing things to you.

I have never lost faith in the people. I know that when the issues were laid before them, they would arise to preserve their liberties. I have not been disappointed. All over the country the people have become aroused. Democracy is on the march, and it's on the march to victory!

I have only one request to make of you: vote on election day. Vote for yourselves. You don't have to vote for me. Vote in your own interests. And when you do that, you can only vote one way — vote for the welfare of the country, vote for the welfare of the world, and vote for your own welfare by voting the Democratic ticket straight on November 2.

NOTE: During his address the president referred to former governor Alfred E. Smith, Senator Robert F. Wagner, and former governor Herbert Lehman, all of New York. Later he referred to Senator Robert A. Taft of Ohio.

OCTOBER 29

Address at the Brooklyn Academy of Music
New York City (9:30 P.M.)

Thank you — thank you very, very much. I have had the most cordial and warmest welcome that any man could wish for, and I thank you from the bottom of my heart. All of Greater New York has given me a wonderful reception, and Brooklyn makes it unanimous.

I have good news for you. We have the Republicans on the run. All we have to do now is to see that everybody gets to the polls on election day. I want everybody who is listening to me tonight just to make me one promise. I want you to promise that you will vote and that you will make sure that your neighbor votes too.

Help your neighbor. Help get him to the polls. This is a crusade for the people, and the way to win is to win it with votes.

Before I say anything else, I would like to pay tribute to a man who is not here tonight. He's not here, because he's out fighting for you, fighting shoulder to shoulder with me in this great crusade. And I'd like to pay tribute to my good friend and running mate, Senator Alben Barkley.

Senator Barkley has been working hard, making a terrific fight to help tell the people of this country the facts of life. He's doing a splendid job, and I want all of you to know that he's your friend and he's working for you. What's more, he's been fighting for you, and he and I together will go on fighting for you.

We said we would tell the people of this country the truth in this campaign, and we have done it. The American people know that we believe in them. They know that we trust them. And they have responded. All they wanted was to have somebody talk to them about the issues.

The Republican candidate wouldn't tell them. He didn't dare.

When Senator Barkley and I started out, there wasn't a newspaper in the country that would have given a plugged nickel for our chance to win this election for the people. But we are going to win it!

Now they're beginning to sing another tune. That's because we are going to win. The Democratic Party is going to win, because you are going to vote.

This night marks the end of my campaign in the East. And the East is with us. A few weeks ago the papers said Massachusetts was in the bag for the Republicans. That just isn't so. Massachusetts is going Democratic by one hundred thousand votes. Rhode Island is Democratic. Connecticut is going Democratic by forty thousand, and as for New York—well, you tell me. Is New York going Democratic? Of course it is! New York State is going to turn in a good old-fashioned Democratic majority, just as it did four times in a row for Franklin D. Roosevelt.

Tonight I'm going to talk about how this election affects your chance for peace. In the interest of peace, your Democratic Party has created strong bipartisan support for the kind of foreign policy that would not change over the years. In this task, from the very outset, we have had the cooperation of some wise and patriotic Republicans.

The Democratic Party stands pledged to conduct our foreign policy in the interests of the American people as a whole, without regard to party. Your president and your Democratic administration have scrupulously honored that pledge of bipartisan cooperation in foreign policy. And we are going to keep that pledge, no matter what provocation is offered by the Republican candidate for president.

I had hoped that we would get through this political campaign without the Republican candidate dragging American foreign policy into party politics. But he has seen fit to attack the Democratic Party's record on foreign policy. He has attacked my conduct of foreign affairs in unmeasured terms. He has torn off his mask of bipartisanship and revealed the ugly partisan passion underneath. I feel, therefore, that I would be failing in my duty to bring the issues to the people if I did not discuss the Republican record in the field of foreign affairs.

Let me say at the outset, in a few words, what our American foreign policy is. The heart and soul of American foreign policy is peace. We are supporting a world organization to keep the peace, and a world economic policy to create prosperity for all mankind.

The first and most important feature of our foreign policy is to strengthen the United Nations, which seeks to bring about a peaceful adjustment of differences between nations. Our guiding principle is international cooperation. The very basis of our foreign policy is cooperative action with other nations.

Unfortunately, our hopes for worldwide cooperation have been hampered by the Soviet Union, whose policies and objectives seem to be at odds with what the United States and other democratic nations are striving for. This fact — this disharmony — makes it even more urgent that we act in concert with those nations which are devoted to the same objectives that we are.

We have not deserted — we will never desert — the brave men and women who have rallied to the cause of peace and freedom throughout the world. We will not sacrifice them to totalitarian aggression.

In these matters, a very great responsibility lies upon the president of the United States. While he looks ahead, working for a happy outcome, he must also take thought of possible disasters. The president's responsibility goes far beyond the formalities of diplomacy. It extends to ultimate reality — the final consequence of war and peace.

A president must approach this task humbly and sincerely. He must be sure in his heart that no error, no pride, no arrogance on his part, offers an obstacle to the achievement of peace. The president is the servant of the American people. He must leave no stone unturned in expressing their will for peace.

Throughout the world today the people yearn for peace. If all peoples were free to express themselves as we are, there would be absolutely no danger of war. But, unfortunately, we are confronted by a dangerous and difficult circumstance.

The people of the Soviet Union are surrounded by a curtain of censorship through which very little of the truth about the other people of the world can penetrate. The leaders of the Soviet Union are victims of their own iron curtain. There is a vast amount of misinformation and misunderstanding in the minds of those who control the destinies of the Russian people.

One of the problems which I face, and one of the problems which my great predecessor faced, is to pierce that iron curtain and to get the truth across to the leaders in the Soviet Union. We must try to get them to understand that our people are united in what we think is right, that we have no evil intentions, that we stand firmly behind the United Nations.

Our experience has shown that formal diplomatic channels do not always succeed in doing this. It is the duty of the president, therefore, to consider and study every possible approach to the heart and understanding of the Soviet leaders. I have given this problem prayerful consideration. I shall continue to do so.

There are some misguided persons who believe that further peaceful discussions are useless. But that is not the position of the United States government. So long as I am president of the United States, the door will not be closed to peace. I will always explore every possible means, no matter how difficult or how unconventional, for reaching agreement.

I welcome the abuse that is showered upon me by those who have made up their minds that war is inevitable. In my search for peace, I do not care what epithets may be hurled at me by those who think that we must hurry on to an inevitable catastrophe. I don't care about that. I don't care what they say. There is nothing new they can say about me. It has all been said. And I am here to tell you that the American people don't believe it.

But when the Republican leaders deliberately misinterpret my private consultations with the secretary of state and try to tell the people of America that my constant concern about peace is wrong, then I have to protest about it. I do not believe that war is inevitable, and I shall make use of every honorable means to prevent it.

The way in which our foreign policy has been attacked raises doubts as to the good faith with which the Republican leaders in this campaign are approaching this whole question. Do they regard it as nothing more than a campaign issue? Do they understand that the stakes in this matter are war or peace, life or death, not only for ourselves and our children but for our civilization? These doubts are made more serious by the record which the Republican Party has made in foreign policy over the years.

Let me say right now that I welcome the real contributions made to our foreign policy by certain Republicans in recent years. They have been helpful, and I will always give them full and friendly credit. But these contributions, however real, must not blind us to the fact that the Republican Party, has a party, is a late convert to the cause of international good will and cooperation.

After the First World War, the United States had its first great opportunity to lead the world to peace. I have always believed that it was the will of Almighty God at that time that we should enter into and lead the League of Nations. How much misery and suffering the world would have been spared if we had only followed Woodrow Wilson!

We are not now making the same mistake that was made in 1920. God willing, we will never make that mistake again. God willing, we will never make that mistake again.

In the fateful election of 1920, the Democratic Party urged the people to take the lead in international affairs. The people recognized that this was their duty. But they were betrayed — betrayed by another Republican candidate who campaigned on both sides of the issue, and a Republican Party which sabotaged the ideal of international cooperation as soon as it had won the election.

Why did this happen? It happened because powerful interests in the Republican Party were so selfish and so shortsighted that they blocked our participation in the world effort for peace. And those same interests are still powerful in the Republican Party. Don't let anybody tell you anything different.

Let me give you an example of their influence today. Remember that in the 1920s the Republican Party moved into Washington and enacted the highest tariffs in our history — tariffs that helped bring on World War II.

Then in the 1930s the terrible errors of the Republican high tariff were corrected by the Democratic Party, under the leadership of President Roosevelt and that great secretary of state, Cordell Hull. Using the powerful instrument of reciprocal trade agreements, we have demonstrated the possibility of an expanding world economy. We have provided a new foundation for a prosperous and a peaceful world. But now this foundation is threatened by Republican reaction.

The leader of the Republican high tariff lobby in the 1920s was a gentleman from Pennsylvania by the name of Joe Grundy. That same Mr. Grundy showed up at the Republican Convention in Philadelphia this year and masterminded the choice of the Republican candidate. And his personal protégé is now the Republican chairman of the National Committee. Do you want to return to Grundyism? The Republican Party has served notice that that is what you can expect from them.

This year I sent a message to the Congress asking that the power to conduct the reciprocal trade program be extended another three years. Those Republicans simply crippled the act and extended it for one year instead of the customary three, thinking that next year, if they are successful in this election, they will be able to finish the job.

Let me give you another example. When the European recovery program was before the Senate, the isolationist forces in the Republican Party rose behind Senator Taft in an attempt to slash that program and change it from one of world reconstruction to one of handout relief. It is preposterous for the Republican candidate to say that "Republican statesmanship" — if there is such a thing — changed our original idea of the European recovery program into a practical measure. If it had not been for the experience and wisdom of the Democratic Party in international affairs, the European recovery program would have been mutilated before it was launched.

These are some of the reasons which lead me to believe that our foreign policy is safer in Democratic hands than in Republican hands. These are some of the reasons why the American people would make a mistake if they should entrust the future of our country to a Republican president and a Republican Congress for the next four years.

The Communists would like to see that happen. That is the main reason the Communists are trying so desperately to defeat me. That is why the Communists are supporting a third party. They know that the candidate of the third party will not win a single state, yet the Communists are using him in an effort to defeat me and elect a Republican president.

The Communists know the Republican record, even if the Republicans hope that the rest of us have forgotten it. The Communists regard the Republican Party as the party of inaction, confusion, and rejection — the party that ensures a depression that would both weaken our influence abroad and spread misery at home.

Better still from the Communist point of view, the Republican Party's record shows that it is not free from the forces of isolationism. On the basis of the record, the Communists believe that these forces would control the Republican Party and lead to an American policy of hit-and-run diplomacy.

The Communists want us to get out of Europe and Asia. They want us to stop helping European countries and China. They want us to withdraw and leave the field entirely to them. They know they can never get what they want so long as the Democratic Party remains in control of this government. But the Communists have real reason to hope that Republican isolationism will exert its pressure within the Republican Party, and, in a period of time, they can take over nation after nation.

My friends, that must not happen! We must never withdraw to the Republican isolationism of the 1920s. If you do that, communism will become so powerful that the security of this nation will be gravely endangered.

As the Communists make their crafty plans, they find that on issue after issue they can expect no help from the Democratic Party. But to the Republican Party, however, they see a basic philosophy, a course of action, an attitude toward the future, that fills them with fervent hope.

Make no mistake about it. The fate of mankind depends on the foreign policy of the United States. Grave decisions lie before us. The next Congress will have to decide whether we shall continue our reciprocal trade policy or abolish it. The next Congress will have to decide whether the European recovery program shall be continued. If the forces of reaction and isolation gain control of our government in this election, these fateful issues will be decided the wrong way.

And if they are decided the wrong way, our present great contribution to world peace will end. With it will end the hope for which this generation of mankind has sacrificed so much. The Democratic Party rejects that tragic course.

Now, our foreign policy is a people's foreign policy. Its purpose is to win a people's peace. It demands a people's government in Washington, not a special-interest government. It demands that we maintain here in America a firm democratic base for world democracy. It demands that we maintain here in America a secure economic base for world recovery. These are the issues that we Democrats have brought before the American people in this crusade. And the American people understand those issues. They have responded to the challenge of our time.

Now, I have only one request to make of you. Exercise your right to control this government of yours by doing your duty on election day, getting up there early and voting the straight Democratic ticket, and the country will be safe.

[At this point the president introduced his family. He then resumed speaking.]

I want to say to you most hospitable people in Brooklyn that I have never enjoyed a meeting more in my life, and I never was more serious with anything in my life than what I told you this evening. I am highly honored to be on this platform with so many distinguished Democrats.

NOTE: During his address the president referred to Secretary of State George C. Marshall, former secretary of state Cordell Hull, former senator from Pennsylvania Joseph R. Grundy, and Senator Robert A. Taft of Ohio.

★ ★ ★ ★ ★ ★ ★ ★ ★ ★ ★ ★ ★ ★ ★ ★ ★ ★

OCTOBER 30

Final Campaign Speech

Kiel Auditorium, St. Louis (9:30 P.M.)

Thank you, my friends. I appreciate most highly this reception in St. Louis, but bear in mind that I have got to talk to the whole United States tonight, and you can cheer in between times too.

I can't tell you how very much I appreciate this reception on my return to my home state. It touches my heart — right where I live. I thank the governor most sincerely for this cordial introduction — which nobody heard but the radio audience. But I know that when Missouri feels this way, we are on the road to victory.

On November 2 we are going to have a Democratic governor in Missouri and a Democratic delegation in the Congress of the United States.

I have been in many a campaign, my friends. I have made four strenuous and hard-fought campaigns in the great state of Missouri for United States senator. But never in my lifetime have I been in a campaign, nor seen a campaign, such as I have been through recently. I became president of the United States three years, six months, and eighteen days ago, and we have been through the most momentous period in the history of the world in that time.

Twenty-six days after I became president, Germany surrendered unconditionally. Four months and twenty-one days after I was sworn in as president of the United States, Japan folded up and surrendered unconditionally, thus ending the greatest war in the history of the world. I succeeded to the presidency after one of the greatest Democrats who ever lived in this world had been there for nearly twelve years. I was nominated in Chicago with Franklin Roosevelt in 1944 on the Democratic platform, and I have tried to carry out that platform, and I have tried to carry out that platform since I have been president of the United States.

One of my first and greatest decisions after becoming president of the United States was made just two minutes after I was sworn in, and that was the order that the conference to form the United Nations should go forward in San Francisco on the 25th day of April. That conference went forward to a successful conclusion, and the United Nations is working for the peace and welfare of this world, right now.

Four days after Japan surrendered on September the 2nd, my first policy message went to Congress. That message contained twenty-one points, based on the Democratic platform of 1944, which I had helped to write. When that message went to Congress, the smear campaign on your president started in all its vile and untruthfully slanted headlines, columns, and editorials. Hearst's character assassins, McCormick-Patterson saboteurs — all began firing at me, as did the conservative columnists and radio commentators. Not because they believed anything they said or wrote, but because they were paid to do it.

In January 1946, I repeated what I thought the government should do, and I have repeated it time and again since that time — and I haven't changed a bit. I am still the Democrat you nominated in Chicago on the Democratic platform of 1944, and I am still for Roosevelt's New Deal.

Now, those saboteurs and character assassins did a lot better job than they intended to do in 1946. They elected that Republican "do-nothing" 80th Congress. And then the issues were clearly drawn. We know where the Republicans stand, and we know where the Democrats stand, and I brought those issues to the country, my friends.

I have traveled up and down this nation twenty-two thousand miles since the campaign started, and ninety-one hundred miles on a nonpolitical campaign before the campaign started.

I have told the people that there is just one big issue in this campaign and that's the people against the special interests. The Republicans stand for special interests, and they always have. The Democratic Party, which I now head, stands for the people — and always has stood for the people.

In 1932 the farmers in this great nation were being foreclosed and were going broke at a terrific rate. I think, in 1932, 123,000 farmers were evicted from their farms. The net farm income that year was $2½ billion. The total income was $4½ billion. In 1947 the gross income of the farmers was $30 billion, and the net income was $18 billion. In 1947 there were less than eight hundred farm foreclosures. The Democratic Party is responsible for that result, and nothing else!

And I'll say to you that any farmer in these United States who votes against his own interests, that is, who votes the Republican ticket, ought to have his head examined!

One of the first things that this Republican, "do-nothing" 80th Congress did was to hamstring the Commodity Credit Corporation, so they couldn't make price support loans to the farmers. When I was over here in Illinois about a month ago, corn was selling down there in southern Illinois at 47 cents below what the support price ought to be, because the Commodity Credit Corporation could not furnish the bins in which to store that corn. That's a provision that the Republicans put in the Commodity Credit Corporation charter when they renewed it. That's how they love the farmers! They want to bust them just like they did in 1932.

When the Democrats took over in 1933, labor was at its lowest ebb. Labor unions had a very small membership at that time — about three million. And there were twelve million people walking up and down the streets in this country, hunting for jobs that they couldn't get.

And one of the first things that the Democratic administration did was to inaugurate a charter for labor, a bill of rights for labor, known as the Wagner Labor Relations Act. And under that Wagner Labor Relations Act, the wages of labor are three times what they were in 1932 and 1933. There are sixty-one million people at work in this country. And jobs are hunting for people, not people hunting for jobs. And that's the result of Democratic policy.

And one of the first bills introduced in this "do-nothing" Republican 80th Congress was to cripple the Wagner Labor Relations Act. That Taft-Hartley law was passed over my veto. That bill was passed over my veto, and it was passed with the idea, so the Republican leaders in the Congress said, of putting labor in its place. They wanted to take the bargaining power away from labor, so it could not deal with industry on a fair basis.

Do you know how that came about? That came about, because two-thirds of the people in 1946 decided that they did not have an interest in their government, and two-thirds of them didn't vote. Most laboring men stayed away from the polls in 1946 — and see what they got! They got the Taft-Hartley Act.

Now, I am advising you, as I have advised every audience to whom I have spoken in these United States, that your duty — you owe a duty to the government, because the government is yours, when you exercise that power to vote. And if you don't vote on November the 2nd, and you send back an 81st Congress under the same leadership that the 80th Congress had, you will be in some fix sure enough — because the Republicans have already said what they are going to do to labor if they get control of the government.

Now, one of the laws which was passed in that period of Democratic administrations was the minimum wage law. That minimum wage law was intended to put a floor under wages, and it put a floor of 40 cents an hour under wages. That was the Fair Labor Standards Act, and it limited the hours which could be worked to 40 hours a week, and it eliminated child labor.

I have been trying to get this 80th Congress, ever since January 3, 1947, when it met the first time, to raise that standard — that floor under wages — to 75 cents an hour. They refused to do that. And I thought maybe a remedy would be if I could manage it — and I can, of course — that I would like to see those Republican congressional leaders try to live in Washington on $16 a week and support a family.

The Democrats have believed always that the welfare of the whole people should come first, and that means that the farmers, labor, small businessmen, and everybody else in the country should have a fair share of the prosperity that goes around. We have placed the farmers in the best position they have ever been in the history of the world. We have placed labor in its best position it has ever been in the history of the world. And we have been against monopoly from the start.

Now, when farmers are prosperous, and when labor gets good wages, business is bound to be good. And that is the reason the national income is higher in this country than it has ever been before in the history of the world.

You know, these Republican old dealers — these fellows, these special-privilege fellows — try to tell the farmers that labor is getting too much pay and that is the reason for the high cost of living. And they tell the laborers that the farmers are getting too much for their crops, and that is the reason for the high cost of living.

Well, I will tell you what the reason is: it's the fellow in between who is getting too much profit. That's what the difficulty is.

The income of the real corporations in 1932 was $3 billion minus, on the red side of the ledger. In 1947 it was $17 billion plus, on the right side of the ledger. And the Democrats brought that about too — don't let anybody tell you anything different about that.

Now, I asked in this twenty-one-point program, which I referred to in the beginning, for a housing bill. Three years ago, I asked for that housing bill. That was the bill known as the Wagner-Ellender-Taft bill. That bill was a housing bill which was in the interests of all the people. It was mainly fixed to help low-income people to clear slums and to help the cities get low-rent housing. Well, that bill was killed in the House of Representatives. And then, in 1947, it was reintroduced, and it was known as the Taft-Ellender-Wagner bill — you see, they reversed it a little bit.

I sent message after message to the Congress to get that bill passed. Well, they didn't pass it. They passed a fake housing bill, a housing bill which was intended to build no housing. And they are trying to make you believe they passed a housing bill.

Of all the fake campaigns, this one is the tops, so far as the Republican candidate for president is concerned. He has been following me up and down this country making speeches about home and mother and unity and efficiency and things of that kind. He won't talk about the issues, but he did let his foot slip when he endorsed the 80th Congress. He endorsed that Congress! He said that Congress had done great things for the future of this country.

It has done great things for the special interests in this country. It has worked for the lobbies. The worst lobby outfits in the history of the United States have been in Washington, surrounding that 80th Congress. And they haven't done a thing that these good-for-nothing lobbies haven't asked them to do. The reason they couldn't get that housing bill was because the real estate lobby was sitting by the rat hole and wouldn't let it come out of the committee.

I asked that Congress to do something about high prices. In fact, I called them back into special session twice and begged them with everything I had to do something about the inflationary price spiral that is going on. Oh, no, they couldn't do that. But they could pass a rich man's tax bill, a tax bill that benefited the fellow at the top income bracket but didn't do the poor boys any good.

I want to show you why they passed that bill. I will read you one of their campaign documents, which is a record of what the Republicans believe in. Now, that rich man's tax bill, which I vetoed three times — and they had to pass it three times before they could make a law out of it — gave a fellow who was getting $60 a week a savings of about $1.58 a week. And the price spiral has taken that all away from him, and it has gone on out through the roof and taken some of his savings away from him too.

But that same tax bill gave the fellow who was getting $100,000 a year $16,658.44 in savings. That is four times the net salary of the president of the United States!

Well, you know why they did that? Here is what this thing said: "There's Money in Your Pocket!" — now, this is a document put out in a number of states to the Republican state committees. "The Republican 80th Congress Reduced Your Income Tax. The following table shows your approximate savings under the new tax savings law effective May 1, 1948." That is after I vetoed it three times.

Now, listen to this — this is outrageous — this is one of the most terrible political documents ever I saw. Now, listen to it: "Do you want more of this sort of constructive — *constructive* — government action? Then use your tax savings to make a substantial investment in a Republican victory." In other words, you fellows that are getting all these savings on this tax income thing that we gave you, send it to us so that we spend it to beat the Democrats! That is literally what that means.

Now, there is another issue between me and this Congress on which we didn't agree, and that was education. There was an education bill to help the states introduced into this Congress, and it passed the Senate. And it provided $300 million to be allocated to the states on the same basis that we allocate the road money to help build roads. But the Republican leadership in the House of Representatives wouldn't let the House vote on that bill.

They are not interested in whether teachers have good pay or not. They are not interested in whether the kids get a proper education or not. They don't care if there are seventy-five or eighty kids in one room and one teacher to look after them at a salary that is not a living wage. They are not interested in that.

I want to say to you that I think it is just as important to see that these children get the proper sort of place to go to school, and the proper sort of teachers to teach them, as it is to build roads for them to ride in buses over the roads to school.

Then I asked this Congress to do something about the health of the people of this country. I asked them for health insurance. I asked them for hospitals. You know, in this country there are two classes of people that get all the medical care that they ought to have; and that is the fellow who has got a million dollars at this end of the scale, and the fellow that hasn't got a cent at this end. But the people in the middle, the large number of people in the middle between those two classes, can't afford to go to a hospital. They can't afford to pay what it costs sometimes, and they can't afford sometimes even to pay the doctor's bill after they get service.

I wanted an insurance program that would work, so that a fellow would have a little money saved up when it came time to pay medical and hospital bills, and the doctor and the hospital would get paid promptly. But the Republicans are against that. They say that's socialized medicine. Well, it isn't.

That's just good common sense, and some of these days we are going to get it, because the Democrats are going back in power, and we are going to see that we get it.

Now, my friends, I have been all over these United States from one end to another and when I started out, the song was — "Well, you can't win"; "the Democrats can't win." Ninety percent of the press is against us, but that didn't discourage me one little bit. You know, I had four campaigns here in the great state of Missouri, and I never had a metropolitan paper for me that whole time. And I licked them every time!

I have been in San Diego, I have been in Boston, I have been in Seattle, I have been in Miami, I have been in New York, Chicago, and all the county seats nearly and state capitals, and I have never had such a reception as you have given me here tonight. And I think that means something. People are waking up to the fact that this is their government and that they can control their government if they get out and vote on election day. That is all they need to do.

When I was in New York yesterday, and the day before, I had the greatest turnout that has ever happened in that city in its history, so everybody told me — about four and a half million people came out to see what I looked like and to listen to what I had to say. There were a million people on the streets in Chicago, and Ed Kelly told my secretary that there wouldn't be that many people in Boston, because Boston didn't have that many people in it — but there were.

People are waking up that the tide is beginning to roll, and I am here to tell you that if you do your duty as citizens of the greatest republic the sun has ever shone on, we will have a government that will be for your interests, that will be for peace in the world and for the welfare of all the people and not just a few.

NOTE: During his address the president referred to Phil M. Donnelly, governor of Missouri, and Edward J. Kelly, former mayor of Chicago.

★ ★ ★ ★ ★ ★ ★ ★ ★ ★ ★ ★ ★ ★ ★ ★ ★ ★

NOVEMBER I (ELECTION EVE)

Radio Address to the American People

President Truman's Home, Independence,

Missouri (9:37 P.M.)

My fellow citizens:

I want to thank Senator Barkley for his generous introduction and to say what I have said before — that no candidate for president ever had a finer running mate. The people of this country are everlastingly in his debt for his leadership in their interest. Senator Barkley will go down in history as one of our greatest public servants.

During the past two months, the senator and I have been going up and down the country, telling the people what the Democratic Party stands for in government. I have talked in great cities, in state capitals, in county seats, in crossroad villages and country towns.

Everywhere the people showed great interest. They came out by the millions. They wanted to know what the issues were in this campaign, and I told them what was in my mind and in my heart. I explained the meaning of the Democratic Party platform. I told them that I intend to carry it out if they will give me a Democratic Congress to help.

From the bottom of my heart I thank the people of the United States for their cordiality to me and for their interest in the affairs of this great nation and of the world. I trust the people, because when they know the facts, they do the right thing. I have tried to tell them the facts and explain the issues.

Now it is up to you, the people of this great nation, to decide what kind of government you want — whether you want government for all the people or government for just the privileged few.

Tonight I am at my home here in Independence — Independence, Missouri — with Mrs. Truman and Margaret. We are here to vote tomorrow as citizens of this republic. I hope that all of you who are entitled to vote will exercise that great privilege. When you vote, you are in control of your government.

Tomorrow you will be deciding between the principles of the Democratic Party, the party of the people, and the principles of the Republican Party, the party of privilege. Your vote tomorrow is not just a vote for one man or another; it is a vote which will affect you and your families for years to come.

Now, maybe you would like to know why I have made this fight for the people. I will try to tell you. It is a matter of the things I believe in.

I believe in a free America — strong and undivided. I believe in the principles of the Declaration of Independence — that we the people shall govern ourselves through our elected representatives, that every man and woman has a right to an equal voice in the management of our nation's affairs. I believe that the Constitution, which rightly protects property, is still more deeply pledged to protect human rights.

I believe that the Democratic Party is the party of the people. I believe that through the Democratic Party, all classes of our citizens will receive fairer treatment and more security. I believe, in particular, in the industrial workers, the farmers, and the small businessmen of this country. I believe they can best protect themselves against reaction and against inflation through the Democratic Party. I believe that a Democratic administration, pledged to continue the present policies of our country, is our best insurance against going back to the dark days of 1932.

I believe with all my heart and soul that Almighty God has intended the United States of America to lead the world to peace. We were in that position thirty years ago. We failed to meet our obligation then, and World War II was the result. This time we must live up to our opportunity to establish a permanent peace for the greatest age in human history. We have two great goals — one to build a secure life for ourselves here at home, and the other to build a lasting peace for the world.

As you mark your ballots tomorrow, I want every housewife to ask herself: will this protect my home and my children for the future? I want every husband to ask himself: is this best for my wife and family? I want all voters to ask themselves: is this the best way to ensure a free and prosperous country?

And now, my fellow citizens, the future welfare of our country is in your hands. I have told you the truth as God has given me wisdom to see the truth. Go to the polls tomorrow and vote your convictions, your hopes, and your faith — your faith in the future of a nation that under God can lead the world to freedom and to peace.

NOTE: The president was introduced by Senator Alben W. Barkley, vice presidential candidate, who said, "No man called suddenly to the presidency of this nation ever

History's most enduring image of a triumphant underdog. (Mercantile Library Association)

faced a greater task. Whether this task involved our internal economy or the delicate and dangerous course of international relations, it called for the exercise of patience, tolerance, firmness, foresight, and courage. . . . This quiet, modest, patient, courageous, God-fearing, determined man in war and the aftermath of war, at home and abroad, has brought strength to our economy, expansion and permanence to our influence, and hope to hopeless men and women throughout the world. . . ." The address was carried on a nationwide radio broadcast.

NOVEMBER 3

Remarks at the Victory Celebration
Independence, Missouri (8 P.M.)

Mr. Mayor and my fellow townsmen and citizens of this great county named after Andrew Jackson:

I can't tell you how very much I appreciate this turnout to celebrate a victory — not my victory but a victory of the Democratic Party for the people.

I want to inform you, Mr. Mayor, that protocol goes out the window when I am in Independence. I am a citizen of this town and a taxpayer, and I want to be treated just like the rest of the taxpayers in this community are treated, whether you extend the city limits or not.

And I thank you very much indeed for this celebration, which is not for me. It is for the whole country. It is for the whole world, for the simple reason that you have given me tremendous responsibility.

Now, since you have given me that responsibility, I want every single one of you to help carry out that responsibility, for the welfare of this great republic and for the welfare and peace of the world at large. And I am sure that is what you are going to do.

I can't begin to thank the people who are responsible for the Democratic Party winning this great election. Of course, I am indebted to everybody for that win, and I will have to just say to every single one of you individually that I am going to do the very best I can to carry out the Democratic platform, as I promised to do in my speeches over this country.

And we have a Congress now, and I am sure we will make some progress in the next four years.

Thank you all very much.

NOTE: The president's opening words "Mr. Mayor" referred to Mayor Roger T. Sermon of Independence.

Index

Italic page numbers indicate photographs.

Three weeks after the great upset, HST and Bess waved to the crowd at the Army-Navy game in Philadelphia's Municipal Stadium. (Truman Library)

STEVE NEAL is a political columnist for the *Chicago Sun-Times*.

His most recent books include *Eleanor and Harry: The Correspondence of Eleanor Roosevelt and Harry S. Truman* and *Harry and Ike: The Partnership That Remade the Postwar World*. *Rolling on the River: The Best of Steve Neal* is available from Southern Illinois University Press.